Back Again to Paris

Jacques Casanova de Seingalt

[ZHINGOORA BOOKS]

BACK AGAIN TO PARIS

CHAPTER XIII

My Stay at Paris and My Departure for Strasburg, Where I Find the Renaud—My Misfortunes at Munich and My Sad Visit to Augsburg

At ten o'clock in the morning, cheered by the pleasant feeling of being once more in that Paris which is so imperfect, but which is the only true town in the world, I called on my dear Madame d'Urfe, who received me with open arms. She told me that the young Count d'Aranda was quite well, and if I liked she would ask him to dinner the next day. I told her I should be delighted to see him, and then I informed her that the operation by which she was to become a man could not be performed till Querilinto, one of the three chiefs of the Fraternity of the Rosy Cross, was liberated from the dungeons of the Inquisition, at Lisbon.

"This is the reason," I added, "that I am going to Augsburg in the course of next month, where I shall confer with the Earl of Stormont as to the liberation of the adept, under the pretext of a mission from the Portuguese Government. For these purposes I shall require a good letter of credit, and some watches and snuff-boxes to make presents with, as we shall have to win over certain of the profane."

"I will gladly see to all that, but you need not hurry yourself as the
Congress will not meet till September."

"Believe me, it will never meet at all, but the ambassadors of the belligerent powers will be there all the same. If, contrary to my expectation, the Congress is held, I shall be obliged to go to Lisbon. In any case, I promise to see you again in the ensuing winter. The fortnight that I have to spend here will enable me to defeat a plot of St. Germain's."

"St. Germain—he would never dare to return to Paris."

"I am certain that he is here in disguise. The state messenger who ordered him to leave London has convinced him the English minister was not duped by the demand for his person to be given up, made by the Comte d'Afri in the name of the king to the States-General."

All this was mere guess-work, and it will be seen that I guessed rightly.

Madame d'Urfe then congratulated me on the charming girl whom I had sent from Grenoble to Paris. Valenglard had told her the whole story.

"The king adores her," said she, "and before long she will make him a father. I have been to see her at Passi with the Duchesse de l'Oraguais."

"She will give birth to a son who will make France happy, and in thirty years time you will see wondrous things, of which, unfortunately, I can tell you nothing until your transformation. Did you mention my name to her?"

"No, I did not; but I am sure you will be able to see her, if only at Madame Varnier's."

She was not mistaken; but shortly afterwards an event happened which made the madness of this excellent woman much worse.

Towards four o'clock, as we were talking over my travels and our designs, she took a fancy to walk in the Bois du Boulogne. She begged me to accompany her, and I acceded to her request. We walked into the deepest recesses of the wood and sat down under a tree. "It is eighteen years ago," said she, "since I fell asleep on the same spot that we now occupy. During my sleep the divine Horosmadis came down from the sun and stayed with me till I awoke. As I opened my eyes I saw him leave me and ascend to heaven. He left me with child, and I bore a girl which he took away from me years ago, no doubt to punish me for, having so far forgotten myself as to love a mortal after him. My lovely Iriasis was like him."

"You are quite sure that M. d'Urfe was not the child's father?"

"M. d'Urfe did not know me after he saw me lying beside the divine
Anael."

"That's the genius of Venus. Did he squint?"

"To excess. You are aware, then, that he squints?"

"Yes, and I know that at the amorous crisis he ceases to squint."

"I did not notice that. He too, left me on account of my sinning with an
Arab."

"The Arab was sent to you by an enemy of Anael's, the genius of Mercury."

"It must have been so; it was a great misfortune."

"On the contrary, it rendered you more fit for transformation."

We were walking towards the carriage when all at once we saw St. Germain, but as soon as he noticed us he turned back and we lost sight of him.

"Did you see him?" said I. "He is working against us, but our genie makes him tremble."

"I am quite thunderstruck. I will go and impart this piece of news to the Duc de Choiseul to-morrow morning. I am curious to hear what he will say when I tell him."

As we were going back to Paris I left Madame d'Urfe, and walked to the Porte St. Denis to see my brother. He and his wife received me with cries of joy. I thought the wife very pretty but very wretched, for Providence had not allowed my brother to prove his manhood, and she was unhappily in love with him. I say unhappily, because her love kept her faithful to him, and if she had not been in love she might easily have found a cure for her misfortune as her husband allowed her perfect liberty. She grieved bitterly, for she did not know that my brother was impotent, and fancied that the reason of his abstention was that he did not return her love; and the mistake was an excusable one, for he was like a Hercules, and indeed he was one, except where it was most to be desired. Her grief threw her into a consumption of which she died five or six years later. She did not mean her death to be a punishment to her husband, but we shall see that it was so.

The next day I called on Madame Varnier to give her Madame Morin's letter. I was cordially welcomed, and Madame Varnier was kind enough to say that she had rather see me than anybody else in the world; her niece had told her such strange things about me that she had got quite curious. This, as is well known, is a prevailing complaint with women.

"You shall see my niece," she said, "and she will tell you all about herself."

She wrote her a note, and put Madame Morin's letter under the same envelope.

"If you want to know what my niece's answer is," said Madame Varnier, "you must dine with me."

I accepted the invitation, and she immediately told her servant that she was not at home to anyone.

The small messenger who had taken the note to Passi returned at four o'clock with the following epistle:

"The moment in which I see the Chevalier de Seingalt once more will be one of the happiest of my life. Ask him to be at your house at ten o'clock the day after tomorrow, and if he can't come then please let me know."

After reading the note and promising to keep the appointment, I left Madame Varnier and called on Madame de Rumain, who told me I must spend a whole day with her as she had several questions to put to my oracle.

Next day Madame d'Urfe told me the reply she had from the Duc de Choiseul, when she told him that she had seen the Comte de St. Germain in the Bois du Boulogne

"I should not be surprised," said the minister, "considering that he spent the night in my closet."

The duke was a man of wit and a man of the world. He only kept secrets when they were really important ones; very different from those make-believe diplomatists, who think they give themselves importance by making a mystery of trifles of no consequence. It is true that the Duc de Choiseul very seldom thought anything of great importance; and, in point of fact, if there were less intrigue and more truth about diplomacy (as there ought to be), concealment would be rather ridiculous than necessary.

The duke had pretended to disgrace St. Germain in France that he might use him as a spy in London; but Lord Halifax was by no means taken in by this stratagem. However, all governments have the politeness to afford one another these services, so that none of them can reproach the others.

The small Conte d'Aranda after caressing me affectionately begged me to come and breakfast with him at his boarding-house, telling me that Mdlle. Viar would be glad to see me.

The next day I took care not to fail in my appointment with the fair lady. I was at Madame Varnier's a quarter of an hour before the arrival of the dazzling brunette, and I waited for her with a beating at the heart which shewed me that the small favours she had given me had not quenched the flame of love. When she made her appearance the stoutness of her figure carried respect with it, so that I did not feel as if I could come forward and greet her tenderly; but she was far from thinking that more respect was due to her than when she was at Grenoble, poor but also pure. She kissed me affectionately and told me as much.

"They think I am happy," said she, "and envy my lot; but can one be happy after the loss of one's self-respect? For the last six months I have only smiled, not laughed; while at Grenoble I laughed heartily from true gladness. I have diamonds, lace, a beautiful house, a superb carriage, a lovely garden, waiting-maids, and a maid of honour who perhaps despises me; and although the highest Court ladies treat me like a princess, I do not pass a single day without experiencing some mortification."

"Mortification?"

"Yes; people come and bring pleas before me, and I am obliged to send them away as I dare not ask the king anything."

"Why not?"

"Because I cannot look on him as my lover only; he is always my sovereign, too. Ah! happiness is to be sought for in simple homes, not in pompous palaces."

"Happiness is gained by complying with the duties of whatever condition of life one is in, and you must constrain yourself to rise to that exalted station in which destiny has placed you."

"I cannot do it; I love the king and I am always afraid of vexing him. I am always thinking that he does too much for me, and thus I dare not ask for anything for others."

"But I am sure the king would be only too glad to shew his love for you by benefiting the persons in whom you take an interest."

"I know he would, and that thought makes me happy, but I cannot overcome my feeling of repugnance to asking favours. I have a hundred louis a month for pin-money, and I distribute it in alms and presents, but with due economy, so that I am not penniless at the end of the month. I have a foolish notion that the chief reason the king loves me is that I do not importune him."

"And do you love him?"

"How can I help it? He is good-hearted, kindly, handsome, and polite to excess; in short, he possesses all the qualities to captivate a woman's heart.

"He is always asking me if I am pleased with my furniture, my clothes, my servants, and my garden, and if I desire anything altered. I thank him with a kiss, and tell him that I am pleased with everything."

"Does he ever speak of the scion you are going to present to him?"

"He often says that I ought to be careful of myself in my situation. I am hoping that he will recognize my son as a prince of the blood; he ought in justice to do so, as the queen is dead."

"To be sure he will."

"I should be very happy if I had a son. I wish I felt sure that I would have one. But I say nothing about this to anyone. If I dared speak to the king about the horoscope, I am certain he would want to know you; but I am afraid of evil tongues."

"So am I. Continue in your discreet course and nothing will come to disturb your happiness, which may become greater, and which I am pleased to have procured for you."

We did not part without tears. She was the first to go, after kissing me and calling me her best friend. I stayed a short time with Madame Varnier to compose my feelings, and I told her that I should have married her instead of drawing her horoscope.

"She would no doubt have been happier. You did not foresee, perhaps, her timidity and her lack of ambition."

"I can assure you that I did not reckon upon her courage or ambition. I laid aside my own happiness to think only of hers. But what is done cannot be recalled, and I shall be consoled if I see her perfectly happy at last. I hope, indeed, she will be so, above all if she is delivered of a son."

I dined with Madame d'Urfe, and we decided to send back Aranda to his boarding-school that we might be more free to pursue our cabalistic operations; and afterwards I went to the opera, where my brother had made an appointment with me. He took me to sup at Madame Vanloo's, and she received me in the friendliest manner possible.

"You will have the pleasure of meeting Madame Blondel and her husband," said she.

The reader will recollect that Madame Blondel was Manon Baletti, whom I was to have married.

"Does she know I am coming?" I enquired.

"No, I promise myself the pleasure of seeing her surprise."

"I am much obliged to you for not wishing to enjoy my surprise as well. We shall see each other again, but not to-day, so I must bid you farewell; for as I am a man of honour I hope never to be under the same roof as Madame Blondel again."

With this I left the room, leaving everybody in astonishment, and not knowing where to go I took a coach and went to sup with my sister-in-law, who was extremely glad to see me. But all through supper-time this charming woman did nothing but complain of her husband, saying that he had no business to marry her, knowing that he could not shew himself a man.

"Why did you not make the trial before you married?"

"Was it for me to propose such a thing? How should I suppose that such a fine man was impotent? But I will tell you how it all happened. As you know, I was a dancer at the Comedie Italienne, and I was the mistress of M. de Sauci, the ecclesiastical commissioner. He brought your brother to my house, I liked him, and before long I saw that he loved me. My lover advised me that it was an opportunity for getting married and making my fortune. With this idea I conceived the plan of not granting him any favours. He used to come and see me in the morning, and often found me in bed; we talked together, and his passions seemed to be aroused, but it all ended in kissing. On my part, I was waiting for a formal declaration and a proposal of marriage. At that period, M. de Sauci settled an annuity of a thousand crowns on me on the condition that I left the stage.

"In the spring M. de Sauci invited your brother to spend a month in his country house. I was of the party, but for propriety's sake it was agreed that I should pass as your brother's wife. Casanova enjoyed the idea, looking upon it as a jest, and not thinking of the consequences. I was therefore introduced as his wife to my lover's family, as also to his relations, who were judges, officers, and men about town, and to their wives, who were all women of fashion. Your brother was in high glee that to play our parts properly we were obliged to sleep together. For my part, I was far from disliking the idea, or at all events I looked upon it as a short cut to the marriage I desired.

"But how can I tell you? Though tender and affectionate in everything, your brother slept with me for a month without our attaining what seemed the natural result under the circumstances."

"You might have concluded, then, that he was impotent; for unless he were made of stone, or had taken a vow of chastity, his conduct was inexplicable."

"The fact is, that I had no means of knowing whether he was capable or incapable of giving me substantial proof of his love."

"Why did you not ascertain his condition for yourself?"

"A feeling of foolish pride prevented me from putting him to the test. I did not suspect the truth, but imagined reasons flattering to myself. I thought that he loved me so truly that he would not do anything before I was his wife. That idea prevented me humiliating myself by making him give me some positive proof of his powers."

"That supposition would have been tenable, though highly improbable, if you had been an innocent young maid, but he knew perfectly well that your novitiate was long over."

"Very true; but what can you expect of a woman impelled by love and vanity?"

"Your reasoning is excellent, but it comes rather late."

"Well, at last we went back to Paris, your brother to his house, and I to mine, while he continued his courtship, and I could not understand what he meant by such strange behaviour. M. de Sauci, who knew that nothing serious had taken place between us, tried in vain to solve the enigma. 'No doubt he is afraid of getting you with child,' he said, 'and of thus being obliged to marry you.'

I began to be of the same opinion, but I thought it a strange line for a man in love to take.

"M. de Nesle, an officer in the French Guards, who had a pretty wife I had met in the country, went to your brother's to call on me. Not finding me there he asked why we did not live together. Your brother replied openly that our marriage had been a mere jest. M. de Nesle then came to me to enquire if this were the truth, and when he heard that it was he asked me how I would like him to make Casanova marry me. I answered that I should be delighted, and that was enough for him. He went again to your brother, and told him that his wife would never have associated with me on equal terms if I had not been introduced to her as a married woman; that the deceit was an insult to all the company at the country-house, which must be wiped out by his marrying me within the week or by fighting a duel. M. de Nesle added that if he fell he would be avenged by all the gentlemen who had been offended in the same way. Casanova replied, laughing, that so far from fighting to escape marrying me, he was ready to break a lance to get me. 'I love her,' he said, 'and if she loves me I am quite ready to give her my hand. Be kind enough,' he added, 'to prepare the way for me, and I will marry her whenever you like.'

"M. de Nesle embraced him, and promised to see to everything; he brought me the joyful news, and in a week all was over. M. de Nesle gave us a splendid supper on our wedding-day, and since then I have had the title of his wife. It is an empty title, however, for, despite the ceremony and the fatal yes, I am no wife, for your brother is completely impotent. I am an unhappy wretch, and it is all his fault, for he ought to have known his own condition. He has deceived me horribly."

"But he was obliged to act as he did; he is more to be pitied than to be blamed. I also pity you, but I think you are in the wrong, for after his sleeping with you for a month without giving any proof of his manhood you might have guessed the truth. Even if you had been a perfect novice, M. de Sauci ought to have known what was the matter; he must be aware that it is beyond the power of man to sleep beside a pretty woman, and to press her naked body to his breast without becoming, in spite of himself, in a state which would admit of no concealment; that is, in case he were not impotent."

"All that seems very reasonable, but nevertheless neither of us thought of it; your brother looks such a Hercules."

"There are two remedies open to you; you can either have your marriage annulled, or you can take a lover; and I am sure that my brother is too reasonable a man to offer any opposition to the latter course."

"I am perfectly free, but I can neither avail myself of a divorce nor of a lover; for the wretch treats me so kindly that I love him more and more, which doubtless makes my misfortune harder to bear."

The poor woman was so unhappy that I should have been delighted to console her, but it was out of the question. However, the mere telling of her story had afforded her some solace, and after kissing her in such a way as to convince her that I was not like my brother, I wished her good night.

The next day I called on Madame Vanloo, who informed me that Madame Blondel had charged her to thank me for having gone away, while her husband wished me to know that he was sorry not to have seen me to express his gratitude.

"He seems to have found his wife a maid, but that's no fault of mine; and Manon Baletti is the only person he ought to be grateful to. They tell me that he has a pretty baby, and that he lives at the Louvre, while she has another house in the Rue Neuve-des-Petits-Champs."

"Yes, but he has supper with her every evening."

"It's an odd way of living."

"I assure you it answers capitally. Blondel regards his wife as his mistress. He says that that keeps the flame of love alight, and that as he never had a mistress worthy of being a wife, he is delighted to have a wife worthy of being a mistress."

The next day I devoted entirely to Madame de Rumain, and we were occupied with knotty questions till the evening. I left her well pleased. The marriage of her daughter, Mdlle. Cotenfau, with M. de Polignac, which took place five or six years later, was the result of our cabalistic calculations.

The fair stocking-seller of the Rue des Prouveres, whom I had loved so well, was no longer in Paris. She had gone off with a M. de Langlade, and her husband was inconsolable. Camille was ill. Coralline had become the titulary mistress of the Comte de la Marche, son of the Prince of Conti, and the issue of this union was a son, whom I knew twenty years later. He called himself the Chevalier de Montreal, and wore the cross of the Knights of Malta. Several other girls I had known were widowed and in the country, or had become inaccessible in other ways.

Such was the Paris of my day. The actors on its stage changed as rapidly as the fashions.

I devoted a whole day to my old friend Baletti, who had left the theatre and married a pretty ballet-girl on the death of his father; he was making experiments with a view to finding the philosopher's stone.

I was agreeably surprised at meeting the poet Poinsinet at the Comedic Francaise. He embraced me again and again, and told me that M. du Tillot had overwhelmed him with kindness at Parma.

"He would not get me anything to do," said Poinsinet, "because a French poet is rather at a discount in Italy."

"Have you heard anything of Lord Lismore?"

"Yes, he wrote to his mother from Leghorn, telling her that he was going to the Indies, and that if you had not been good enough to give him a thousand Louis he would have been a prisoner at Rome."

"His fate interests me extremely, and I should be glad to call on his lady-mother with you."

"I will tell her that you are in Paris, and I am sure that she will invite you to supper, for she has the greatest desire to talk to you."

"How are you getting on here? Are you still content to serve Apollo?"

"He is not the god of wealth by any means. I have no money and no room, and I shall be glad of a supper, if you will ask me. I will read you my play, the 'Cercle', which has been accepted. I am sure it will be successful?"

The 'Cercle' was a short prose play, in which the poet satirised the jargon of Dr. Herrenschwand, brother of the doctor I had consulted at Soleure. The play proved to be a great success.

I took Poinsinet home to supper, and the poor nursling of the muses ate for four. In the morning he came to tell me that the Countess of Lismore expected me to supper.

I found the lady, still pretty, in company with her aged lover, M. de St. Albin, Archbishop of Cambrai, who spent all the revenues of his see on her. This worthy prelate was one of the illegitimate children of the Duc d'Orleans, the famous Regent, by an actress. He supped with us, but he only opened his mouth to eat, and his mistress only spoke of her son, whose talents she lauded to the skies, though he was in reality a mere scamp; but I felt in duty bound to echo what she said. It would have been cruel to contradict her. I promised to let her know if I saw anything more of him.

Poinsinet, who was heartless and homeless, as they say, spent the night in my room, and in the morning I gave him two cups of chocolate and some money wherewith to get a lodging. I never saw him again, and a few years after he was drowned, not in the fountain of Hippocrene, but in the Guadalquivir. He told me that he had spent a week with M. de Voltaire, and that he had hastened his return to Paris to obtain the release of the Abbe Morellet from the Bastile.

I had nothing more to do at Paris, and I was only waiting for some clothes to be made and for a cross of the order, with which the Holy Father had decorated me, to be set with diamonds and rubies.

I had waited for five or six days when an unfortunate incident obliged me to take a hasty departure. I am loth to write what follows, for it was all my own fault that I was nearly losing my life and my honour. I pity those simpletons who blame fortune and not themselves for their misfortunes.

I was walking in the Tuileries at ten o'clock in the morning, when I was unlucky enough to meet the Dangenancour and another girl. This Dangenancour was a dancer at the opera-house, whom I had desired to meet previously to my last departure from Paris. I congratulated myself on the lucky chance which threw her in my way, and accosted her, and had not much trouble in inducing her to dine with me at Choisi.

We walked towards the Pont-Royal, where we took a coach. After dinner had been ordered we were taking a turn in the garden, when I saw a carriage stop and two adventurers whom I knew getting out of it, with two girls, friends of the ones I had with me. The wretched landlady, who was standing at the door, said that if we liked to sit down together she could give us an excellent dinner, and I said nothing, or rather I assented to the yes of my two nymphs. The dinner was excellent, and after the bill was paid, and we were on the point of returning to Paris, I noticed that a ring, which I had taken off to shew to one of the adventurers named Santis, was still missing. It was an exceedingly pretty miniature, and the diamond setting had cost me twenty-five Louis. I politely begged Santis to return me the ring, and he replied with the utmost coolness that he had done so already.

"If you had returned it," said I, "it would be on my finger, and you see that it is not."

He persisted in his assertion; the girls said nothing, but Santis's friend, a Portuguese, named Xavier, dared to tell me that he had seen the ring returned.

"You're a liar," I exclaimed; and without more ado I took hold of Santis by the collar, and swore I would rot let him go till he returned me my ring. The Portuguese rose to come to his friend's rescue, while I stepped back and drew my sword, repeating my determination not to let them go. The landlady came on the scene and began to shriek, and Santis asked me to give him a few words apart. I thought in all good faith that he was ashamed to restore the ring before company, but that he would give it me as soon as we were alone. I sheathed my sword, and told him to come with me. Xavier got into the carriage with the four girls, and they all went back to Paris.

Santis followed me to the back of the inn, and then assuming a pleasant smile he told me that he had put the ring into his friend's pocket for a joke, but that I should have it back at Paris.

"That's an idle tale," I exclaimed, "your friend said that he saw you return it, and now he has escaped me. Do you think that I am green enough to be taken in by this sort of thing? You're a couple of robbers."

So saying, I stretched out my hand for his watch-chain, but he stepped back and drew his sword. I drew mine, and we had scarcely crossed swords when he thrust, and I parrying rushed in and ran him through and through. He fell to the ground calling, "Help!" I sheathed my sword, and, without troubling myself about him, got into my coach and drove back to Paris.

I got down in the Place Maubert, and walked by a circuitous way to my hotel. I was sure that no one could have come after me there, as my landlord did not even know my name.

I spent the rest of the day in packing up my trunks, and after telling Costa to place them on my carriage I went to Madame d'Urfe. After I had told her of what had happened, I begged her, as soon as that which she had for me was ready, to send it to me at Augsburg by Costa. I should have told her to entrust it to one of her own servants, but my good genius had left me that day. Besides I did not look upon Costa as a thief.

When I got back to the hotel I gave the rascal his instructions, telling him to be quick and to keep his own counsel, and then I gave him money for the journey.

I left Paris in my carriage, drawn by four hired horses, which took me as far as the second post, and I did not stop till I got to Strasburg, where I found Desarmoises and my Spaniard.

There was nothing to keep me in Strasburg, so I wanted to cross the Rhine immediately; but Desarmoises persuaded me to come with him to see an extremely pretty woman who had only delayed her departure for Augsburg in the hope that we might journey there together.

"You know the lady," said the false marquis, "but she made me give my word of honour that I would not tell you. She has only her maid with her, and I am sure you will be pleased to see her."

My curiosity made me give in. I followed Desarmoises, and came into a room where I saw a nice-looking woman whom I did not recognize at first. I collected my thoughts, and the lady turned out to be a dancer whom I had admired on the Dresden boards eight years before. She was then mistress to Count Bruhl, but I had not even attempted to win her favour. She had an excellent carriage, and as she was ready to go to Augsburg I immediately concluded that we could make the journey together very pleasantly.

After the usual compliments had passed, we decided on leaving for Augsburg the following morning. The lady was going to Munich, but as I had no business there we agreed that she should go by herself.

"I am quite sure," she said, afterwards, "that you will come too, for the ambassadors do not assemble at Augsburg till next September."

We supped together, and next morning we started on our way; she in her carriage with her maid, and I in mine with Desarmoises, preceded by Le Duc on horseback. At Rastadt, however, we made a change, the Renaud (as she was called) thinking that she would give less opportunity for curious surmises by riding with me while Desarmoises went with the servant. We soon became intimate. She told me about herself, or pretended to, and I told her all that I did not want to conceal. I informed her that I was an agent of the Court of Lisbon, and she believed me, while, for my part, I believed that she was only going to Munich and Augsburg to sell her diamonds.

We began to talk about Desarmoises, and she said that it was well enough for me to associate with him, but I should not countenance his styling himself marquis.

"But," said I, "he is the son of the Marquis Desarmoises, of Nancy."

"No, he isn't; he is only a retired messenger, with a small pension from the department of foreign affairs. I know the Marquis Desarmoises; he lives at Nancy, and is not so old as our friend."

"Then one can't see how he can be Desarmoises's father."

"The landlord of the inn at Strasburg knew him when he was a messenger."

"How did you make his acquaintance?"

"We met at the table d'hote. After dinner he came up to my room, and told me he was waiting for a gentleman who was going to Augsburg, and that we might make the journey together. He told me the name, and after questioning him I concluded that the gentleman was yourself, so here we are, and I am very glad of it. But listen to me; I advise you to drop all false styles and titles. Why do you call yourself Seingalt?"

"Because it's my name, but that doesn't prevent my old friends calling me Casanova, for I am both. You understand?"

"Oh, yes! I understand. Your mother is at Prague, and as she doesn't get her pension on account of the war, I am afraid she must be rather in difficulties."

"I know it, but I do not forget my filial duties. I have sent her some money."

"That's right. Where are you going to stay at Augsburg?"

"I shall take a house, and if you like you shall be the mistress and do the honours."

"That would be delightful! We will give little suppers, and play cards all night."

"Your programme is an excellent one."

"I will see that you get a good cook; all the Bavarian cooks are good. We shall cut a fine figure, and people will say we love each other madly."

"You must know, dearest, that I do not understand jokes at the expense of fidelity."

"You may trust me for that. You know how I lived at Dresden."

"I will trust you, but not blindly, I promise you. And now let us address each other in the same way; you must call me tu. You must remember we are lovers."

"Kiss me!"

The fair Renaud did not like traveling by night; she preferred to eat a good supper, to drink heavily, and to go to bed just as her head began to whirl. The heat of the wine made her into a Bacchante, hard to appease; but when I could do no more I told her to leave me alone, and she had to obey.

When we reached Augsburg we alighted at the "Three Moors," but the landlord told us that though he could give us a good dinner he could not put us up, as the whole of the hotel had been engaged by the French ambassador. I called on M. Corti, the banker to whom I was accredited, and he soon got me a furnished house with a garden, which I took for six months. The Renaud liked it immensely.

No one had yet arrived at Augsburg. The Renaud contrived to make me feel that I should be lonely at Augsburg without her, and succeeded in persuading me to come with her to Munich. We put up at the "Stag," and made ourselves very comfortable, while Desarmoises went to stay somewhere else. As my business and that of my new mate had nothing in common, I gave her a servant and a carriage to herself, and made myself the same allowance.

The Abbe Gama had given me a letter from the Commendatore Almada for Lord Stormont, the English ambassador at the Court of Bavaria. This nobleman being then at Munich I hastened to deliver the letter. He received me very well, and promised to do all he could as soon as he had time, as Lord Halifax had told him all about it. On leaving his Britannic Lordship's I called on M. de Folard, the French ambassador, and gave him a letter from M. de Choiseul. M. de Folard gave me a hearty welcome, and asked me to dine with him the next day, and the day after introduced me to the Elector.

During the four fatal weeks I spent at Munich, the ambassador's house was the only one I frequented. I call these weeks fatal, and with reason, for in then I lost all my money, I pledged jewels (which I never recovered) to the amount of forty thousand francs, and finally I lost my health. My assassins were the Renaud and Desarmoises, who owed me so much and paid me so badly.

The third day after my arrival I had to call on the Dowager Electress of Saxony. It was my brother-in-law, who was in her train, that made me go, by telling me that it must be done, as she knew me and had been enquiring for me. I had no reason to repent of my politeness in going, as the Electress gave me a good reception, and made me talk to any extent. She was extremely curious, like most people who have no employment, and have not sufficient intelligence to amuse themselves.

I have done a good many foolish things in the course of my existence. I confess it as frankly as Rousseau, and my Memoirs are not so egotistic as those of that unfortunate genius; but I never committed such an act of folly as I did when I went to Munich, where I had nothing to do. But it was a crisis in my life. My evil genius had made me commit one folly after another since I left Turin. The evening at Lord Lismore's, my connection with Desarmoises, my party at Choisi, my trust in Costa, my union with the Renaud, and worse than all, my folly in letting myself play at faro at a place where the knavery of the gamesters is renowned all over Europe, followed one another in fatal succession. Among the players was the famous, or rather infamous, Affisio, the friend of the Duc de Deux-Ponts, whom the duke called his aide-decamp, and who was known for the keenest rogue in the world.

I played every day, and as I often lost money on my word of honour, the necessity of paying the next day often caused me the utmost anxiety. When I had exhausted my credit with the bankers, I had recourse to the Jews who require pledges, and in this Desarmoises and the Renaud were my agents, the latter of whom ended by making herself mistress of all my property. This was not the worst thing she did to me; for she, gave me a disease, which devoured her interior parts and left no marks outwardly, and was thus all the more dangerous, as the freshness of her complexion seemed to indicate the most perfect health. In short, this serpent, who must have come from hell to destroy me, had acquired such a mastery over me that she persuaded me that she would be dishonoured if I called in a doctor during our stay at Munich, as everybody knew that we were living together as man and wife.

I cannot imagine what had become of my wits to let myself be so beguiled, while every day I renewed the poison that she had poured into my veins.

My stay at Munich was a kind of curse; throughout that dreadful month I seemed to have a foretaste of the pains of the damned. The Renaud loved gaming, and Desarmoises was her partner. I took care not to play with them, for the false marquis was an unmitigated cheat and often tricked with less skill than impudence. He asked disreputable people to my house and treated them at my expense; every evening scenes of a disgraceful character took place.

The Dowager Electress mortified me extremely by the way she addressed me on my last two visits to her.

"Everybody knows what kind of a life you lead here, and the way the Renaud behaves, possibly without your knowing it. I advise you to have done with her, as your character is suffering."

She did not know what a thraldom I was under. I had left Paris for a month, and I had neither heard of Madame d'Urfe nor of Costa. I could not guess the reason, but I began to suspect my Italian's fidelity. I also feared lest my good Madame d'Urfe might be dead or have come to her senses, which would have come to the same thing so far as I was concerned; and I could not possibly return to Paris to obtain the information which was so necessary both for calming my mind and refilling my purse.

I was in a terrible state, and my sharpest pang was that I began to experience a certain abatement of my vigors, the natural result of advancing years. I had no longer that daring born of youth and the knowledge of one's strength, and I was not yet old enough to have learnt how to husband my forces. Nevertheless, I made an effort and took a sudden leave of my mistress, telling her I would await her at Augsburg. She did not try to detain me, but promised to rejoin me as soon as possible; she was engaged in selling her jewellery. I set out preceded by Le Duc, feeling very glad that Desarmoises had chosen to stay with the wretched woman to whom he had introduced me. When I reached my pretty house at Augsburg I took to my bed, determined not to rise till I was cured or dead. M. Carli, my banker, recommended to me a doctor named Cephalides, a pupil of the famous Fayet, who had cured me of a similar complaint several years before. This Cephalides was considered the best doctor in Augsburg. He examined me and declared he could cure me by sudorifics without having recourse to the knife. He began his treatment by putting me on a severe regimen, ordering baths, and applying mercury locally. I endured this treatment for six weeks, at the end of which time I found myself worse than at the beginning. I had become terribly thin, and I had two enormous inguinal tumours. I had to make up my mind to have them lanced, but though the operation nearly killed me it did not to make me any better. He was so clumsy as to cut the artery, causing great loss of blood which was arrested with difficulty, and would have proved fatal if it had not been for the care of M. Algardi, a Bolognese doctor in the service of the Prince-Bishop of Augsburg.

I had enough of Cephalides, and Dr. Algardi prepared in my presence eighty-six pills containing eighteen grains of manna. I took one of these pills every morning, drinking a large glass of curds after it, and in the evening I had another pill with barley water, and this was the only sustenance I had. This heroic treatment gave me back my health in two months and a half, in which I suffered a great deal of pain; but I did not begin to put on flesh and get back my strength till the end of the year.

It was during this time that I heard about Costa's flight with my diamonds, watches, snuff-box, linen, rich suits, and a hundred louis which Madame d'Urfe had given him for the journey. The worthy lady sent me a bill of exchange for fifty thousand francs, which she had happily not entrusted to the robber, and the money rescued me very opportunely from the state to which my imprudence had reduced me.

At this period I made another discovery of an extremely vexatious character; namely, that Le Duc had robbed me. I would have forgiven him if he had not forced me to a public exposure, which I could only have avoided with the loss of my honour. However, I kept him in my service till my return to Paris at the commencement of the following year.

Towards the end of September, when everybody knew that the Congress would not take place, the Renaud passed through Augsburg with Desarmoises on her way to Paris; but she dared not come and see me for fear I should make her return my goods, of which she had taken possession without telling me. Four or five years later she married a man named Bohmer, the same that gave the Cardinal de Rohan the famous necklace, which he supposed was destined for the unfortunate Marie Antoinette. The Renaud was at Paris when I returned, but I made no endeavour to see her, as I wished, if possible, to forget the past. I had every reason to do so, for amongst all the misfortunes I had gone through during that wretched year the person I found most at fault was myself. Nevertheless, I would have given myself the pleasure of cutting off Desarmoises's ears; but the old rascal, who, no doubt, foresaw what kind of treatment I was likely to mete to him, made his escape. Shortly after, he died miserably of consumption in Normandy.

My health had scarcely returned, when I forgot all my woes and began once more to amuse myself. My excellent cook, Anna Midel, who had been idle so long, had to work hard to satisfy my ravenous appetite. My landlord and pretty Gertrude, his daughter, looked at me with astonishment as I ate, fearing some disastrous results. Dr. Algardi, who had saved my life, prophesied a dyspepsia which would bring me to the tomb, but my need of food was stronger than his arguments, to which I paid no kind of attention; and I was right, for I required an immense quantity of nourishment to recover my former state, and I soon felt in a condition to renew my sacrifices to the deity for whom I had suffered so much.

I fell in love with the cook and Gertrude, who were both young and pretty. I imparted my love to both of them at once, for I had foreseen that if I attacked them separately I should conquer neither. Besides, I felt that I had not much time to lose, as I had promised to sup with Madame, d'Urfe on the first night of the year 1761 in a suite of rooms she had furnished for me in the Rue de

Bac. She had adorned the rooms with superb tapestry made for Rene of Savoy, on which were depicted all the operations of the Great Work. She wrote to me that she had heard that Santis had recovered from the wound I had given him, and had been committed to the Bicetre for fraud.

Gertrude and Anna Midel occupied my leisure moments agreeably enough during the rest of my stay at Augsburg, but they did not make me neglect society. I spent my evenings in a very agreeable manner with Count Max de Lamberg, who occupied the position of field-marshal to the prince-bishop. His wife had all the attractions which collect good company together. At this house I made the acquaintance of the Baron von Selentin, a captain in the Prussian service, who was recruiting for the King of Prussia at Augsburg. I was particularly drawn to the Count Lamberg by his taste for literature. He was an extremely learned man, and has published some excellent works. I kept up a correspondence with him till his death, by his own fault, in 1792, four years from the time of my writing. I say by his fault, but I should have said by the fault of his doctors, who treated him mercurially for a disease which was not venereal; and this treatment not only killed him but took away his good name.

His widow is still alive, and lives in Bavaria, loved by her friends and her daughters, who all made excellent marriages.

At this time a miserable company of Italian actors made their appearance in Augsburg, and I got them permission to play in a small and wretched theatre. As this was the occasion of an incident which diverted me, the hero, I shall impart it to my readers in the hope of its amusing them also.

CHAPTER XIV

The Actors—Bassi—The Girl From Strasburg The Female Count—My Return to Paris I Go to Metz—Pretty Raton—The Pretended Countess Lascaris

A woman, ugly enough, but lively like all Italians, called on me, and asked me to intercede with the police to obtain permission for her company to act in Augsburg. In spite of her ugliness she was a poor fellow-countrywoman, and without asking her name, or ascertaining whether the company was good or bad, I promised to do my best, and had no difficulty in obtaining the favour.

I went to the first performance, and saw to my surprise that the chief actor was a Venetian, and a fellow-student of mine, twenty years before, at St. Cyprian's College. His name was Bassi, and like myself he had given up the priesthood. Fortune had made an actor of him, and he looked wretched enough, while I, the adventurer, had a prosperous air.

I felt curious to hear his adventures, and I was also actuated by that feeling of kindliness which draws one towards the companions of one's youthful and especially one's school days, so I went to the back as soon as the curtain fell. He recognized me directly, gave a joyful cry, and after he had embraced me he introduced me to his wife, the woman who had called on me, and to his daughter, a girl of thirteen or fourteen, whose dancing had delighted me. He did not stop here, but turning to his mates, of whom he was chief, introduced me to them as his best friend. These worthy people, seeing me dressed like a lord, with a cross on my breast, took me for a cosmopolitan charlatan who was expected at Augsburg, and Bassi, strange to say, did not undeceive them. When the company had taken off its stage rags and put on its everyday rags, Bassi's ugly wife took me by the arm and said I must come and sup with her. I let myself be led, and we soon got to just the kind of room I had imagined. It was a huge room on the ground floor, which served for kitchen, dining-room, and bedroom all at once. In the middle stood a long table, part of which was covered with a cloth which looked as if it had been in use for a month, and at the other end of the room somebody was washing certain earthenware dishes in a dirty pan. This den was lighted by one candle stuck in the neck of a broken bottle, and as there were no snuffers Bassi's wife snuffed it cleverly with her finger and thumb, wiping her hand on the table-cloth after throwing the burnt wick on the floor. An actor with long moustaches, who played the villain in the various pieces, served an enormous dish of hashed-up meat, swimming in a sea of dirty water dignified with the name of sauce; and the hungry family proceeded to tear pieces of bread off the loaf with their fingers or teeth, and then to dip them in the dish; but as all did the same no one had a right to be disgusted. A large pot of ale passed from hand to hand, and with all this misery mirth displayed itself on every countenance, and I had to ask myself what is happiness. For a second course there was a dish of fried pork, which was devoured with great relish. Bassi was kind enough not to press me to take part in this banquet, and I felt obliged to him.

The meal over, he proceeded to impart to me his adventures, which were ordinary enough, and like those which many a poor devil has to undergo; and while he talked his pretty daughter sat on my knee. Bassi brought his story to an end by saying that he was going to Venice for the carnival, and was sure of making a lot of money. I wished him all the luck he could desire, and on his asking me what profession I followed the fancy took me to reply that I was a doctor.

"That's a better trade than mine," said he, "and I am happy to be able to give you a valuable present."

"What is that?" I asked.

"The receipt for the Venetian Specific, which you can sell at two florins a pound, while it will only cost you four gros."

"I shall be delighted; but tell me, how is the treasury?"

"Well, I can't complain for a first night. I have paid all expenses, and have given my actors a florin apiece. But I am sure I don't know how I am to play to-morrow, as the company has rebelled; they say they won't act unless I give each of them a florin in advance."

"They don't ask very much, however."

"I know that, but I have no money, and nothing to pledge; but they will be sorry for it afterwards, as I am sure I shall make at least fifty florins to-morrow."

"How many are there in the company?"

"Fourteen, including my family. Could you lend me ten florins? I would pay you back tomorrow night."

"Certainly, but I should like to have you all to supper at the nearest inn to the theatre. Here are the ten florins."

The poor devil overflowed with gratitude, and said he would order supper at a florin a head, according to my instructions. I thought the sight of fourteen famished actors sitting down to a good supper would be rather amusing.

The company gave a play the next evening, but as only thirty or at most forty people were present, poor Bassi did not know where to turn to pay for the lighting and the orchestra. He was in despair; and instead of returning my ten florins he begged me to lend him another ten, still in the hope of a good house next time. I consoled him by saying we would talk it over after supper, and that I would go to the inn to wait for my guests.

I made the supper last three hours by dint of passing the bottle freely. My reason was that I had taken a great interest in a young girl from Strasburg, who played singing chamber-maids. Her features were exquisite and her voice charming, while she made me split my sides with laughing at her Italian pronounced with an Alsatian accent, and at her gestures which were of the most comic description.

I was determined to possess her in the course of the next twenty-four hours, and before the party broke up I spoke as follows:—

"Ladies and gentlemen, I will engage you myself for a week at fifty florins a day on the condition that you acknowledge me as your manager for the time being, and pay all the expenses of the theatre. You must charge the prices I name for seats, five members of the company to be chosen by me must sup with me every evening. If the receipts amount to more than fifty florins, we will share the overplus between us."

My proposal was welcomed with shouts of joy, and I called for pen, ink, and paper, and drew up the agreement.

"For to-morrow," I said to Bassi, "the prices for admission shall remain the same, but the day after we will see what can be done. You and your family will sup with me to-morrow, as also the young Alsatian whom I could never separate from her dear Harlequin."

He issued bills of an enticing description for the following evening; but, in spite of all, the pit only contained a score of common people, and nearly all the boxes were empty.

Bassi had done his best, and when we met at supper he came up to me looking extremely confused, and gave me ten or twelve florins.

"Courage!" said I; and I proceeded to share them among the guests present.

We had a good supper, and I kept them at table till midnight, giving them plenty of choice wine and playing a thousand pranks with Bassi's daughter and the young Alsatian, who sat one on each side of me. I did not heed the jealous Harlequin, who seemed not to relish my familiarities with his sweetheart. The latter lent herself to my endearments with a bad enough grace, as she hoped Harlequin would marry her, and consequently did not want to vex him. When supper was over, we rose, and I took her between my arms, laughing, and caressing her in a manner which seemed too suggestive to the lover, who tried to pull me away. I thought this rather too much in my turn, and seizing him by his shoulders I dismissed him with a hearty kick, which he received with great humility. However, the situation assumed a melancholy aspect, for the poor girl began to weep bitterly. Bassi and his wife, two hardened sinners, laughed at her tears, and Bassi's daughter said that her lover had offered me great provocation; but the young Alsatian continued weeping, and told me that she would never sup with me again if I did not make her lover return.

"I will see to all that," said I; and four sequins soon made her all smiles again. She even tried to shew me that she was not really cruel, and that she would be still less so if I could manage the jealous Harlequin. I promised everything, and she did her best to convince me that she would be quite complaisant on the first opportunity.

I ordered Bassi to give notice that the pit would be two florins and the boxes a ducat, but that the gallery would be opened freely to the first comers.

"We shall have nobody there," said he, looking alarmed.

"Maybe, but that remains to be seen. You must request twelve soldiers to keep order, and I will pay for them."

"We shall want some soldiers to look after the mob which will besiege the gallery, but as for the rest of the house . . . ."

"Again I tell you, we shall see. Carry out my instructions, and whether they prove successful or no, we will have a merry supper as usual."

The next day I called upon the Harlequin in his little den of a room, and with two Louis, and a promise to respect his mistress, I made him as soft as a glove.

Bassi's bills made everybody laugh. People said he must be mad; but when it was ascertained that it was the lessee's speculation, and that I was the lessee, the accusation of madness was turned on me, but what did I care? At night the gallery was full an hour before the rise of the curtain; but the pit was empty, and there was nobody in the boxes with the exception of Count Lamberg, a Genoese abbe named Bolo, and a young man who appeared to me a woman in disguise.

The actors surpassed themselves, and the thunders of applause from the gallery enlivened the performance.

When we got to the inn, Bassi gave me the three ducats for the three boxes, but of course I returned them to him; it was quite a little fortune for the poor actors. I sat down at table between Bassi's wife and daughter, leaving the Alsatian to her lover. I told the manager to persevere in the same course, and to let those laugh who would, and I made him promise to play all his best pieces.

When the supper and the wine had sufficiently raised my spirits, I devoted my attention to Bassi's daughter, who let me do what I liked, while her father and mother only laughed, and the silly Harlequin fretted and fumed at not being able to take the same liberties with his Dulcinea. But at the end of supper, when I had made the girl in a state of nature, I myself being dressed like Adam before he ate the fatal apple, Harlequin rose, and taking his sweetheart's arm was going to draw her away. I imperiously told him to sit down, and he obeyed me in amazement, contenting himself with turning his back. His sweetheart did not follow his example, and so placed herself on the pretext of defending my victim that she increased my enjoyment, while my vagrant hand did not seem to displease her.

The scene excited Bassi's wife, and she begged her husband to give her a proof of his love for her, to which request he acceded, while modest Harlequin sat by the fire with his head on his hands. The Alsatian was in a highly excited state, and took advantage of her lover's position to grant me all I wished, so I proceeded to execute the great work with her, and the violent movements of her body proved that she was taking as active a part in it as myself.

When the orgy was over I emptied my purse on the table, and enjoyed the eagerness with which they shared a score of sequins.

This indulgence at a time when I had not yet recovered my full strength made me enjoy a long sleep. Just as I awoke I was handed a summons to appear before the burgomaster. I made haste with my toilette, for I felt curious to know the reason of this citation, and I was aware I had nothing to fear. When I appeared, the magistrate addressed me in German, to which I turned a deaf ear, for I only knew enough of that language to ask for necessaries. When he was informed of my ignorance of German he addressed me in Latin, not of the Ciceronian kind by any means, but in that peculiar dialect which obtains at most of the German universities.

"Why do you bear a false name?" he asked.

"My name is not false. You can ask Carli, the banker, who has paid me fifty thousand florins."

"I know that; but your name is Casanova, so why do you call yourself
Seingalt?"

"I take this name, or rather I have taken it, because it belongs to me, and in such a manner that if anyone else dared to take it I should contest it as my property by every legitimate resource."

"Ah! and how does this name belong to you?"

"Because I invented it; but that does not prevent my being Casanova as well."

"Sir, you must choose between Casanova and Seingalt; a man cannot have two names."

"The Spaniards and Portuguese often have half a dozen names."

"But you are not a Spaniard or a Portuguese; you are an Italian: and, after all, how can one invent a name?"

"It's the simplest thing in the world."

"Kindly explain."

"The alphabet belongs equally to the whole human race; no one can deny that. I have taken eight letters and combined them in such a way as to produce the word Seingalt. It pleased me, and I have adopted it as my surname, being firmly persuaded that as no one had borne it before no one could deprive me of it, or carry it without my consent."

"This is a very odd idea. Your arguments are rather specious than well grounded, for your name ought to be none other than your father's name."

"I suggest that there you are mistaken; the name you yourself bear because your father bore it before you, has not existed from all eternity; it must have been invented by an ancestor of yours who did not get it from his father, or else your name would have been Adam. Does your worship agree to that?"

"I am obliged to; but all this is strange, very strange."

"You are again mistaken. It's quite an old custom, and I engage to give you by to-morrow a long list of names invented by worthy people still living, who are allowed to enjoy their names in peace and quietness without being cited to the town hall to explain how they got them."

"But you will confess that there are laws against false names?"

"Yes, but I repeat this name is my true name. Your name which I honour, though I do not know it, cannot be more true than mine, for it is possible that you are not the son of the gentleman you consider your father." He smiled and escorted me out, telling me that he would make enquiries about me of M. Carli.

I took the part of going to M. Carli's myself. The story made him laugh. He told me that the burgomaster was a Catholic, a worthy man, well to do, but rather thick-headed; in short, a fine subject for a joke.

The following morning M. Carli asked me to breakfast, and afterwards to dine with the burgomaster.

"I saw him yesterday," said he, "and we had a long talk, in the course of which I succeeded in convincing him on the question of names, and he is now quite of your opinion."

I accepted the invitation with pleasure, as I was sure of seeing some good company. I was not undeceived; there were some charming women and several agreeable men. Amongst others, I noticed the woman in man's dress I had seen at the theatre. I watched her at dinner, and I was the more convinced that she was a woman. Nevertheless, everybody addressed her as a man, and she played the part to admiration. I, however, being in search of amusement, and not caring to seem as if I were taken in, began to talk to her in a stream of gallantry as one talks to a woman, and I contrived to let her know that if I were not sure of her sex I had very strong

45

suspicions. She pretended not to understand me, and everyone laughed at my feigned expression of offence.

After dinner, while we were taking coffee, the pretended gentleman shewed a canon who was present a portrait on one of her rings. It represented a young lady who was in the company, and was an excellent likeness—an easy enough matter, as she was very ugly. My conviction was not disturbed, but when I saw the imposter kissing the young lady's hand with mingled affection and respect, I ceased jesting on the question of her sex. M. Carli took me aside for a moment, and told me that in spite of his effeminate appearance this individual was a man, and was shortly going to marry the young lady whose hand he had just kissed.

"It may be so," said I, "but I can't believe it all the same."

However, the pair were married during the carnival, and the husband obtained a rich dowry with his wife. The poor girl died of 'grief in the course of a year, but did not say a word till she was on her death-bed. Her foolish parents, ashamed of having been deceived so grossly, dared not say anything, and got the female swindler out of the way; she had taken good care, however, to lay a firm hold on the dowry. The story became known, and gave the good folk of Augsburg much amusement, while I became renowned for my sagacity in piercing the disguise.

I continued to enjoy the society of my two servants and of the fair Alsation, who cost me a hundred louis. At the end of a week my agreement with Bassi came to an end, leaving him with some money in his pocket. He continued to give performances, returning to the usual prices and suppressing the free gallery. He did very fair business.

I left Augsburg towards the middle of December.

I was vexed on account of Gertrude, who believed herself with child, but could not make up her mind to accompany me to France. Her father would have been pleased for me to take her; he had no hopes of getting her a husband, and would have been glad enough to get rid of her by my making her my mistress.

We shall hear more of her in the course of five or six years, as also of my excellent cook, Anna Midel, to whom I gave a present of four hundred florins. She married shortly afterwards, and when I visited the town again I found her unhappy.

I could not make up my mind to forgive Le Duc, who rode on the coachman's box, and when we were in Paris, half-way along the Rue St. Antoine, I made him take his trunk and get down; and I left him there without a character, in spite of his entreaties. I never heard of him again, but I still miss him, for, in spite of his great failings, he was an excellent servant. Perhaps I should have called to mind the important services he had rendered me at Stuttgart, Soleure, Naples, Florence, and Turin; but I could not pass over his impudence in compromising me before the Augsburg magistrate. If I had not succeeded in bringing a certain theft home to him, it would have been laid to my door, and I should have been dishonoured.

I had done a good deal in saving him from justice, and, besides, I had rewarded him liberally for all the special services he had done me.

From Augsburg I went to Bale by way of Constance, where I stayed at the dearest inn in Switzerland. The landlord, Imhoff, was the prince of cheats, but his daughters were amusing, and after a three days' stay I continued my journey. I got to Paris on the last day of the year 1761, and I left the coach at the house in the Rue du Bacq, where my good angel Madame d'Urfe had arranged me a suite of rooms with the utmost elegance.

I spent three weeks in these rooms without going anywhere, in order to convince the worthy lady that I had only returned to Paris to keep my word to her, and make her be born again a man.

We spent the three weeks in making preparations for this divine operation, and our preparations consisted of devotions to each of the seven planets on the days consecrated to each of the intelligences. After this I had to seek, in a place which the spirits would point out to me, for a maiden, the daughter of an adept, whom I was to impregnate with a male child in a manner only known to the Fraternity of the Rosy Cross. Madame d'Urfe was to receive the child into her arms the moment it was born; and to keep it beside her in bed for seven days. At the end of the seven days she would die with her lips on the lips of the child, who would thus receive her reasonable soul, whereas before it had only possessed a vegetal soul.

This being done, it was to be my part to care for the child with the magisterium which was known to me, and as soon as it had attained to its third year Madame d'Urfe would begin to recover her self-consciousness, and then I was to begin to initiate her in the perfect knowledge of the Great Work.

The operation must take place under the full moon during the months of April, May, or June. Above all, Madame d'Urfe was to make a will in favour of the child, whose guardian I was to be till its thirteenth year.

This sublime madwoman had no doubts whatever as to the truth of all this, and burned with impatience to see the virgin who was destined to be the vessel of election. She begged me to hasten my departure.

I had hoped, in obtaining my answers from the oracle, that she would be deterred by the prospect of death, and I reckoned on the natural love of life making her defer the operation for an indefinite period. But such was not the case, and I found myself obliged to keep my word, in appearance at all events, and to go on my quest for the mysterious virgin.

What I wanted was some young hussy whom I could teach the part, and I thought of the Corticelli. She had been at Prague for the last nine months, and when we were at Bologna I had promised to come and see her before the end of the year. But as I was leaving Germany—by no means a land of pleasant memories to me—I did not think it was worth while going out of my way for such a trifle in the depth of winter. I resolved to send her enough money for the journey, and to let her meet me in some French town.

M. de Fouquet, a friend of Madame d'Urfe's, was Governor of Metz, and I felt sure that, with a letter of introduction from Madame d'Urfe, this nobleman would give me a distinguished reception. Besides, his nephew, the Comte de Lastic, whom I knew well, was there with his regiment. For these reasons I chose Metz as a meeting-place with the virgin Corticelli, to whom this new part would certainly be a surprise. Madame d'Urfe gave me the necessary introductions, and I left Paris on January 25th, 1762, loaded with presents. I had a letter of credit to a large amount, but I did not make use of it as my purse was abundantly replenished.

I took no servant, for after Costa's robbing me and Le Duc's cheating me I felt as if I could not trust in anyone. I got to Metz in two days, and put up at the "Roi Dagobert," an excellent inn, where I found the Comte de Louvenhaupt, a Swede, whom I had met at the house of the Princess of Anhalt-Zerbst, mother of the Empress of Russia. He asked me to sup with him and the Duc de Deux Ponts, who was travelling incognito to Paris to visit Louis XV., whose constant friend he was.

The day after my arrival I took my letters to the governor, who told me I must dine with him every day. M. de Lastic had left Metz, much to my regret, as he would have contributed in no small degree to the pleasure of my stay. The same day I wrote to the Corticelli, sending her fifty louis, and telling her to come with her mother as soon as possible, and to get someone who knew the way to accompany her. She could not leaves Prague before the beginning of Lent, and to make sure of her coming I promised that I would make her fortune.

In four or five days I knew my way about the town, but I did not frequent polite assemblies, preferring to go to the theatre, where a comic opera singer had captivated me. Her name was Raton, and she was only fifteen, after the fashion of actresses who always subtract at least two or three years from their age. However, this failing is common to women, and is a pardonable one, since to be youthful is the greatest of all advantages to them. Raton was not so much handsome as attractive, but what chiefly made her an object of desire was the fact that she had put the price of twenty-five louis on her maidenhead. One could spend a night with her, and make the trial for a Louis; the twenty-five were only to be paid on the accomplishment of the great work.

It was notorious that numerous officers in the army and young barristers had undertaken the operation unsuccessfully, and all of them had paid a louis apiece.

This singular case was enough to whet my curiosity. I was not long before I called on Raton, but not wishing to be duped by her I took due precautions. I told her that she must come and sup with me, and that I would give her the twenty-five louis if my happiness was complete, and that if I were unsuccessful she should have six louis instead of one, provided that she was not tied. Her aunt assured me that this was not the case; but I could not help thinking of Victorine.

Raton came to supper with her aunt, who went to bed in an adjoining closet when the dessert was brought in. The girl's figure was exquisitely beautiful, and I felt that I had no small task before me. She was kind, laughing, and defied me to the conquest of a fleece not of gold, but of ebony, which the youth of Metz had assaulted in vain. Perhaps the reader will think that I, who was no longer in my first vigour, was discouraged by the thought of the many who had failed; but I knew my powers, and it only amused me. Her former lovers had been Frenchmen, more skilled in carrying strong places by assault than in eluding the artfulness of a girl who corked herself up. I was an Italian, and knew all about that, so I had no doubts as to my victory.

However, my preparations were superfluous; for as soon as Raton felt from my mode of attack that the trick would be of no avail she met my desires half-way, without trying the device which had made her seem to be what she was no longer to her inexpert lovers. She gave herself up in good faith, and when I had promised to keep the secret her ardours were equal to mine. It was not her first trial, and I consequently need not have given her the twenty-five louis, but I was well satisfied, and not caring much for maidenheads rewarded her as if I had been the first to bite at the cherry.

I kept Raton at a louis a day till the arrival of the Corticelli, and she had to be faithful to me, as I never let her go out of my sight. I liked the girl so well and found her so pleasant that I was sorry that the Corticelli was coming; however, I was told of her arrival one night just as I was leaving my box at the theatre. My footman told me in a loud voice that my lady wife, my daughter, and a gentleman had just arrived from Frankfort, and were awaiting me at the inn.

"Idiot," I exclaimed, "I have no wife and no daughter."

However, all Metz heard that my family had arrived.

The Corticelli threw her arms round my neck, laughing as usual, and her mother presented me to the worthy man who had accompanied them from Prague to Metz. He was an Italian named Month, who had lived for a long time at Prague, where he taught his native language. I saw that M. Month and the old woman were suitably accommodated, and I then led the young fool into my room. I found her changed for the better; she had grown, her shape was improved, and her pleasant manners made her a very charming girl.

CHAPTER XV

I Returned to Paris With The Corticelli, Now Countess Lascaris— The Hypostasis Fails—Aix-la-Chapelle—Duel—Mimi d'Ache—The Corticelli Turns Traitress to Her Own Disadvantage—Journey to Sulzbach

"Why did you allow your mother to call herself my wife, little simpleton? Do you think that's a compliment to my judgment? She might have given herself out for your governess, as she wishes to pass you off as my daughter."

"My mother is an obstinate old woman who had rather be whipped at the cart-tail than call herself my governess. She has very narrow ideas, and always thinks that governess and procuress mean the same thing."

"She's an old fool, but we will make her hear reason either with her will or in spite of it. But you look well dressed, have you made your fortune?"

"At Prague I captivated the affections of Count N——, and he proved a generous lover. But let your first action be to send back M. Month. The worthy man has his family at Prague to look after; he can't afford to stay long here."

"True, I will see about it directly."

The coach started for Frankfort the same evening, and summoning Month I thanked him for his kindness and paid him generously, so he went off well pleased.

I had nothing further to do at Metz, so I took leave of my new friends, and in two days time I was at Nancy, where I wrote to Madame d'Urfe that I was on my way back with a virgin, the last of the family of Lascaris, who had once reigned at Constantinople. I begged her to receive her from my hands, at a country house which belonged to her, where we should be occupied for some days in cabalistic ceremonies.

She answered that she would await us at Pont-Carre, an old castle four leagues distant from Paris, and that she would welcome the young princess with all possible kindness.

"I owe her all the more friendship," added the sublime madwoman, "as the family of Lascaris is connected with the family of d'Urfe, and as I am to be born again in the seed of the happy virgin."

I felt that my task would be not exactly to throw cold water on her enthusiasm, but to hold it in check and to moderate its manifestations. I therefore explained to her by return of post that she must be content to treat the virgin as a countess, not a princess, and I ended by informing her that we should arrive, accompanied by the countess's governess, on the Monday of Holy Week.

I spent twelve days at Nancy, instructing the young madcap in the part she had to play, and endeavouring to persuade her mother that she must content herself with being the Countess Lascaris's humble servant. It was a task of immense difficulty; it was not enough to shew her that our success depended on her submitting; I had to threaten to send her back to Bologna by herself. I had good reason to repent of my perseverance. That woman's obstinacy was an inspiration of my good angel's, bidding me avoid the greatest mistake I ever made.

On the day appointed we reached Pont-Carre. Madame d'Urfe, whom I had advised of the exact hour of our arrival, had the drawbridge of the castle lowered, and stood in the archway in the midst of her people, like a general surrendering with all the honours of war. The dear lady, whose madness was but an excess of wit, gave the false princess so distinguished a reception that she would have shewn her amazement if I had not warned her of what she might expect. Thrice did she clasp her to her breast with a tenderness that was quite maternal, calling her her beloved niece, and explaining the entire pedigrees of the families of Lascaris and d'Urfe to make the countess understand how she came to be her niece. I was agreeably surprised to see the polite and dignified air with which the Italian wench listened to all this; she did not even smile, though the scene must have struck her as extremely laughable.

As soon as we got into the castle Madame d'Urfe proceeded to cense the new-comer, who received the attention with all the dignity of an opera queen, and then threw herself into the arms of the priestess, who received her with enthusiastic affection.

At dinner the countess was agreeable and talkative, which won her Madame d'Urfe's entire favour; her broken French being easily accounted for. Laura, the countess's mother, only knew her native Italian, and so kept silence. She was given a comfortable room, where her meals were brought to her, and which she only left to hear mass.

The castle was a fortified building, and had sustained several sieges in the civil wars. As its name, Pont-Carre, indicated, it was square, and was flanked by four crenelated towers and surrounded by a broad moat. The rooms were vast, and richly furnished in an old-fashioned way. The air was full of venomous gnats who devoured us and covered our faces with painful bites; but I had agreed to spend a week there, and I should have been hard put to it to find a pretext for shortening the time. Madame d'Urfe had a bed next, her own for her niece, but I was not afraid of her attempting to satisfy herself as to the countess's virginity, as the oracle had expressly forbidden it under pain or failure. The operation was fixed for the fourteenth day of the April moon.

On that day we had a temperate supper, after which I went to bed. A quarter of an hour afterwards Madame d'Urfe came, leading the virgin Lascaris. She undressed her, scented her, cast a lovely veil over her body, and when the countess was laid beside me she remained, wishing to be present at an operation which was to result in her being born again in the course of nine months.

The act was consummated in form, and then Madame d'Urfe left us alone for the rest of the night, which was well employed. Afterwards, the countess slept with her aunt till the last day of the moon, when I asked the oracle if the Countess Lascaris had conceived. That well might be, for I had spared nothing to that intent; but I thought it more prudent to make the oracle reply that the operation had failed because the small Count d'Aranda had watched us behind a screen. Madame d'Urfe was in despair, but I consoled her by a second reply, in which the oracle declared that though the operation could only be performed in France in April, it could take place out of that realm in May; but the inquisitive young count, whose influence had proved so fatal, must be sent for at least a year to some place a hundred leagues from Paris. The oracle also indicated the manner in which he was to travel; he was to have a tutor, a servant, and all in order.

The oracle had spoken, and no more was wanted. Madame d'Urfe thought of an abbe she liked for his tutor, and the count was sent to Lyons, with strong letters of commendation to M. de Rochebaron, a relation of his patroness. The young man was delighted to travel, and never had any suspicion of the way in which I had slandered him. It was not a mere fancy which suggested this course of action. I had discovered that the Corticelli was making up to him, and that her mother favoured the intrigue. I had surprised her twice in the young man's room, and though he only cared for the girl as a youth cares for all girls, the Signora Laura did not at all approve of my opposing her daughter's designs.

Our next task was to fix on some foreign town where we could again attempt the mysterious operation. We settled on Aix-la-Chapelle, and in five or six days all was ready for the journey.

The Corticelli, angry with me for having thwarted her in her projects, reproached me bitterly, and from that time began to be my enemy; she even allowed herself to threaten me if I did not get back the pretty boy, as she called him.

"You have no business to be jealous," said she, "and I am the mistress of my own actions."

"Quite right, my dear," I answered; "but it is my business to see that you do not behave like a prostitute in your present position."

The mother was in a furious rage, and said that she and her daughter would return to Bologna, and to quiet them I promised to take them there myself as soon as we had been to Aix-la-Chapelle.

Nevertheless I did not feel at ease, and to prevent any plots taking place I hastened our departure.

We started in May, in a travelling carriage containing Madame d'Urfe, myself, the false Lascaris, and her maid and favourite, named Brougnole. We were followed by a coach with two seats; in it were the Signora Laura and another servant. Two men-servants in full livery sat on the outside of our travelling carriage. We stopped a day at Brussels, and another at Liege. At Aix there were many distinguished visitors, and at the first ball we attended Madame d'Urfe presented the Lascaris to two Princesses of Mecklenburg as her niece. The false countess received their embraces with much ease and modesty, and attracted the particular attention of the Margrave of Baireuth and the Duchess of Wurtemberg, his daughter, who took possession of her, and did not leave her till the end of the ball.

I was on thorns the whole time, in terror lest the heroine might make some dreadful slip. She danced so gracefully that everybody gazed at her, and I was the person who was complimented on her performance.

I suffered a martyrdom, for these compliments seemed to be given with malicious intent. I suspected that the ballet-girl had been discovered beneath the countess, and I felt myself dishonoured. I succeeded in speaking privately to the young wanton for a moment, and begged her to dance like a young lady, and not like a chorus girl; but she was proud of her success, and dared to tell me that a young lady might know how to dance as well as a professional dancer, and that she was not going to dance badly to please me. I was so enraged with her impudence, that I would have cast her off that instant if it had been possible; but as it was not, I determined that her punishment should lose none of its sharpness by waiting; and whether it be a vice or a virtue, the desire of revenge is never extinguished in my heart till it is satisfied.

The day after the ball Madame d'Urfe presented her with a casket containing a beautiful watch set with brilliants, a pair of diamond ear-rings, and a ring containing a ruby of fifteen carats. The whole was worth sixty thousand francs. I took possession of it to prevent her going off without my leave.

In the meanwhile I amused myself with play and making bad acquaintances. The worst of all was a French officer, named d'Ache, who had a pretty wife and a daughter prettier still. Before long the daughter had taken possession of the heart which the Corticelli had lost, but as soon as Madame d'Ache saw that I preferred her daughter to herself she refused to receive me at her house.

I had lent d'Ache ten Louis, and I consequently felt myself entitled to complain of his wife's conduct; but he answered rudely that as I only went to the house after his daughter, his wife was quite right; that he intended his daughter to make a good match, and that if my intentions were honourable I had only to speak to the mother. His manner was still more offensive than his words, and I felt enraged, but knowing the brutal drunken characteristics of the man, and that he was always ready to draw cold steel for a yes or a no, I was silent and resolved to forget the girl, not caring to become involved with a man like her father.

I had almost cured myself of my fancy when, a few days after our conversation, I happened to go into a billiard-room where d'Ache was playing with a Swiss named Schmit, an officer in the Swedish army. As soon as d'Ache saw me he asked whether I would lay the ten Louis he owed me against him.

"Yes," said I, "that will make double or quits."

Towards the end of the match d'Ache made an unfair stroke, which was so evident that the marker told him of it; but as this stroke made him the winner, d'Ache seized the stakes and put them in his pocket without heeding the marker or the other player, who, seeing himself cheated before his very eyes, gave the rascal a blow across the face with his cue. D'Ache parried the blow with his hand, and drawing his sword rushed at Schmit, who had no arms. The marker, a sturdy young fellow, caught hold of d'Ache round the body, and thus prevented murder. The Swiss went out, saying,

"We shall see each other again."

The rascally Frenchman cooled down, and said to me,

"Now, you see, we are quits."

"Very much quits."

"That's all very well; but, by God! you might have prevented the insult which has dishonoured me."

"I might have done so, but I did not care to interfere. You are strong enough to look after yourself. Schmit had not his sword, but I believe him to be a brave man; and he will give you satisfaction if you will return him his money, for there can be no doubt that you lost the match."

An officer, named de Pyene, took me up and said that he himself would give me the twenty louis which d'Ache had taken, but that the Swiss must give satisfaction. I had no hesitation in promising that he would do so, and said I would bring a reply to the challenge the next morning.

I had no fears myself. The man of honour ought always to be ready to use the sword to defend himself from insult, or to give satisfaction for an insult he has offered. I know that the law of duelling is a prejudice which may be called, and perhaps rightly, barbarous, but it is a prejudice which no man of honour can contend against, and I believed Schmit to be a thorough gentleman.

I called on him at day-break, and found him still in bed. As soon as he saw me, he said,

"I am sure you have come to ask me to fight with d'Ache. I am quite ready to burn powder with him, but he must first pay me the twenty Louis he robbed me of."

"You shall have them to-morrow, and I will attend you. D'Ache will be seconded by M. de Pyene."

"Very good. I shall expect you at day-break."

Two hours after I saw de Pyene, and we fixed the meeting for the next day, at six o'clock in the morning. The arms were to be pistols. We chose a garden, half a league from the town, as the scene of the combat.

At day-break I found the Swiss waiting for me at the door of his lodgings, carolling the 'ranz-des-vaches', so dear to his fellow-countrymen. I thought that a good omen.

"Here you are," said he; "let us be off, then."

On the way, he observed, "I have only fought with men of honour up to now, and I don't much care for killing a rascal; it's hangman's work."

"I know," I replied, "that it's very hard to have to risk one's life against a fellow like that."

"There's no risk," said Schmit, with a laugh. "I am certain that I shall kill him."

"How can you be certain?"

"I shall make him tremble."

He was right. This secret is infallible when it is applied to a coward. We found d'Ache and de Pyene on the field, and five or six others who must have been present from motives of curiosity.

D'Ache took twenty louis from his pocket and gave them to his enemy, saying,

"I may be mistaken, but I hope to make you pay dearly for your brutality." Then turning to me he said,

"I owe you twenty louis also;" but I made no reply.

Schmit put the money in his purse with the calmest air imaginable, and making no reply to the other's boast placed himself between two trees, distant about four paces from one another, and drawing two pistols from his pocket said to d'Ache,

"Place yourself at a distance of ten paces, and fire first. I shall walk to and fro between these two trees, and you may walk as far if you like to do so when my turn comes to fire."

Nothing could be clearer or more calmly delivered than this explanation.

"But we must decide," said I, "who is to have the first shot."

"There is no need," said Schmit. "I never fire first, besides, the gentleman has a right to the first shot."

De Pyene placed his friend at the proper distance and then stepped aside, and d'Ache fired on his antagonist, who was walking slowly to and fro without looking at him. Schmit turned round in the coolest manner possible, and said,

"You have missed me, sir; I knew you would. Try again."

I thought he was mad, and that some arrangement would be come to; but nothing of the kind. D'Ache fired a second time, and again missed; and Schmit, without a word, but as calm as death, fired his first pistol in the air, and then covering d'Ache with his second pistol hit him in the forehead and stretched him dead on the ground. He put back his pistols into his pocket and went off directly by himself, as if he were merely continuing his walk. In two minutes I followed his example, after ascertaining that the unfortunate d'Ache no longer breathed.

I was in a state of amazement. Such a duel was more like a combat of romance than a real fact. I could not understand it; I had watched the Swiss, and had not noticed the slightest change pass over his face.

I breakfasted with Madame d'Urfe, whom I found inconsolable. It was the full moon, and at three minutes past four exactly I ought to perform the mysterious creation of the child in which she was to be born again. But the Lascaris, on whom the work was to be wrought, was twisting and turning in her bed, contorting herself in such a way that it would be impossible for me to accomplish the prolific work.

My grief, when I heard what had happened, was hypocritical; in the first place because I no longer felt any desire for the girl, and in the second because I thought I saw a way in which I could make use of the incident to take vengeance on her.

I lavished consolations on Madame d'Urfe; and on consulting the oracle I found that the Lascaris had been defiled by an evil genius, and that I must search for another virgin whose purity must be under the protection of more powerful spirits. I saw that my madwoman was perfectly happy with this, and I left her to visit the Corticelli, whom I found in bed with her mother beside her.

"You have convulsions, have you, dearest?" said I.

"No, I haven't. I am quite well, but all the same I shall have them till you give me back my jewel-casket."

"You are getting wicked, my poor child; this comes of following your mother's advice. As for the casket, if you are going to behave like this, probably you will have it."

"I will reveal all."

"You will not be believed; and I shall send you back to Bologna without letting you take any of the presents which Madame d'Urfe has given you."

"You ought to have given me back the casket when I declared myself with child."

Signora Laura told me that this was only too true, though I was not the father.

"Who is, then?" I asked.

"Count N——, whose mistress she was at Prague."

It did not seem probable, as she had no symptoms of pregnancy; still it might be so. I was obliged to plot myself to bring the plots of these two rascally women to nought, and without saying anything to them I shut myself up with Madame d'Urfe to enquire of the oracle concerning the operation which was to make her happy.

After several answers, more obscure than any returned from the oracular tripod at Delphi, the interpretation of which I left to the infatuated Madame d'Urfe, she discovered herself—and I took care not to contradict her—that the Countess Lascaris had gone mad. I encouraged her fears, and succeeded in making her obtain from a cabalistic pyramid the statement that the reason the princess had not conceived was that she had been defiled by an evil genius—an enemy of the Fraternity of the Rosy Cross. This put Madame d'Urfe fairly on the way, and she added on her own account that the girl must be with child by a gnome.

She then erected another pyramid to obtain guidance on our quest, and I so directed things that the answer came that she must write to the moon.

This mad reply, which should have brought her to her senses, only made her more crazy than ever. She was quite ecstatic, and I am sure that if I had endeavoured to shew her the nothingness of all this I show have had nothing for my trouble. Her conclusion would probably have been that I was possessed by an evil spirit, and was no longer a true Rosy Cross. But I had no idea of undertaking a cure which would have done me harm and her no 'good. Her chimerical notions made her happy, and the cold naked truth would doubtless have made her unhappy.

She received the order to write to the moon with the greater delight as she knew what ceremonies were to be observed in addressing that planet; but she could not dispense with the assistance of an adept, and I knew she would reckon on me. I told her I should always be ready to serve her, but that, as she knew herself, we should have to wait for the first phase of the new moon. I was very glad to gain time, for I had lost heavily at play, and I could not leave Aix-la-Chapelle before a bill, which I had drawn on M. d'O. of Amsterdam, was cashed. In the mean time we agreed that as the Countess Lascaris had become mad, we must not pay any attention to what she might say, as the words would not be hers but would proceed from the evil spirit who possessed her.

Nevertheless, we determined that as her state was a pitiable one, and should be as much alleviated as possible, she should continue to dine with us, but that in the evening she was to go to her governess and sleep with her.

After having thus disposed of Madame d'Urfe to disbelieve whatever the Corticelli cared to tell her, and to concentrate all her energies on the task of writing to Selenis, the intelligence of the moon, I set myself seriously to work to regain the money I had lost at play; and here my cabala was no good to me. I pledged the Corticelli's casket for a thousand louis, and proceeded to play in an English club where I had a much better chance of winning than with Germans or Frenchmen.

Three or four days after d'Ache's death, his widow wrote me a note begging me to call on her. I found her in company with de Pyene. She told me in a lugubrious voice that her husband had left many debts unsettled, and that his creditors had seized everything she possessed; and—that she was thus unable to pay the expenses of a journey, though she wanted to take her daughter with her to Colmar, and there to rejoin her family.

"You caused my husband's death," she added, "and I ask you to give me a thousand crowns; if you refuse me I shall commence a lawsuit against you, for as the Swiss officer has left, you are the only person I can prosecute."

"I am surprised at your taking such a tone towards me," I replied, coldly, "and were it not for the respect I feel for your misfortune, I should answer as bitterly as you deserve. In the first place I have not a thousand crowns to throw away, and if I had I would not sacrifice my money to threats. I am curious to know what kind of a case you could get up against me in the courts of law. As for Schmit, he fought like a brave gentleman, and I don't think you could get much out of him if he were still here. Good-day, madam."

I had scarcely got fifty paces from the house when I was joined by de Pyene, who said that rather than Madame d'Ache should have to complain of me he would cut my throat on the spot. We neither of us had swords.

"Your intention is not a very flattering one," said I, "and there is something rather brutal about it. I had rather not have any affair of the kind with a man whom I don't know and to whom I owe nothing."

"You are a coward."

"I would be, you mean, if I were to imitate you. It is a matter of perfect indifference to me what opinion you may have on the subject.

"You will be sorry for this."

"Maybe, but I warn you that I never go out unattended by a pair of pistols, which I keep in good order and know how to use." So saying I shewd him the pistols, and took one in my right hand.

At this the bully uttered an oath and we separated.

At a short distance from the place where this scene had occurred I met a Neapolitan named Maliterni, a lieutenant-colonel and aide to the Prince de Condo, commander-in-chief of the French army. This Maliterni was a boon companion, always ready to oblige, and always short of money. We were friends, and I told him what had happened.

"I should be sorry," said I, "to have anything to do with a fellow like de Pyene, and if you can rid me of him I promise you a hundred crowns."

"I daresay that can be managed," he replied, "and I will tell you what I can do to-morrow!"

In point of fact, he brought me news the next day that my cut-throat had received orders from his superior officer to leave Aix-la-Chapelle at day-break, and at the same time he gave me a passport from the Prince de Conde.

I confess that this was very pleasant tidings. I have never feared to cross my sword with any man, though never sought the barbarous pleasure of spilling men's blood; but on this occasion I felt an extreme dislike to a duel with a fellow who was probably of the same caste as his friend d'Ache.

I therefore gave Maliterni my heartiest thanks, as well as the hundred crowns I had promised him, which I considered so well employed that I did not regret their loss.

Maliterni, who was a jester of the first water, and a creature of the Marshal d'Estrees, was lacking neither in wit nor knowledge; but he was deficient in a sense of order and refinement. He was a pleasant companion, for his gaiety was inexhaustible and he had a large knowledge of the world. He attained the rank of field-marshal in 1768, and went to Naples to marry a rich heiress, whom he left a widow a year after.

The day after de Pyene's departure I received a note from Mdlle. d'Ache, begging me, for the sake of her sick mother, to come and see her. I answered that I would be at such a place at such a time, and that she could say what she liked to me.

I found her at the place and time I appointed, with her mother, whose illness, it appeared, did not prevent her from going out. She called me her persecutor, and said that since the departure of her best friend, de Pyene, she did not know where to turn; that she had pledged all her belongings, and that I, who was rich, ought to aid her, if I were not the vilest of men.

"I feel for your condition," I replied, "as I feel your abuse of me; and I cannot help saying that you have shewn yourself the vilest of women in inciting de Pyene, who may be an honest man for all I know, to assassinate me. In fine, rich or not, and though I owe you nothing, I will give you enough money to take your property out of pawn, and I may possibly take you to Colmar myself, but you must first consent to my giving your charming daughter a proof of my affection."

"And you dare to make this horrible proposal to me?"

"Horrible or not, I do make it."

"I will never consent."

"Good day, madam."

I called the waiter to pay him for the refreshments I had ordered, and I gave the girl six double louis, but her proud mother forbade her to accept the money from me. I was not surprised, in spite of her distress; for the mother was in reality still more charming than the daughter, and she knew it. I ought to have given her the preference, and thus have ended the dispute, but who can account for his whims? I felt that she must hate me, for she did not care for her daughter, and it must have humiliated her bitterly to be obliged to regard her as a victorious rival.

I left them still holding the six double louis, which pride or scorn had refused, and I went to the faro-table and decided in sacrificing them to fortune; but that capricious deity, as proud as the haughty widow, refused them, and though I left them on the board for five deals I almost broke the bank. An Englishman, named Martin, offered to go shares with me, and I accepted, as I knew he was a good player; and in the course of eight or ten days we did such good business that I was not only able to take the casket out of pledge and to cover all losses, but made a considerable profit in addition.

About this period, the Corticelli, in her rage against me, had told Madame d'Urfe the whole history of her life, of our acquaintance, and of her pregnancy. But the more truthfully she told her story so much the more did the good lady believe her to be mad, and we often laughed together at the extraordinary fancies of the traitress. Madame d'Urfe put all her trust in the instructions which Selenis would give in reply to her letter.

Nevertheless, as the girl's conduct displeased me, I made her eat her meals with her mother, while I kept Madame d'Urfe company. I assured her that we should easily find another vessel of election, the madness of the Countess Lascaris having made her absolutely incapable of participating in our mysterious rites.

Before long, d'Ache's widow found herself obliged to give me her Mimi; but I won her by kindness, and in such a way that the mother could pretend with decency to know nothing about it. I redeemed all the goods she had pawned, and although the daughter had not yet yielded entirely to my ardour, I formed the plan of taking them to Colmar with Madame d'Urfe. To make up the good lady's mind, I resolved to let that be one of the instructions from the moon, and this she would not only obey blindly but would have no suspicions as to my motive.

I managed the correspondence between Selenis and Madame d'Urfe in the following manner:

On the day appointed, we supped together in a garden beyond the town walls, and in a room on the ground floor of the house I had made all the necessary preparations, the letter which was to fall from the moon, in reply to Madame d'Urfe's epistle, being in my pocket. At a little distance from the chamber of ceremonies I had placed a large bath filled with lukewarm water and perfumes pleasing to the deity of the night, into which we were to plunge at the hour of the moon, which fell at one o'clock.

When we had burnt incense, and sprinkled the essences appropriate to the cult of Selenis, we took off all our clothes, and holding the letter concealed in my left hand, with the right I graciously led Madame d'Urfe to the brink of the bath. Here stood an alabaster cup containing spirits of wine which I kindled, repeating magical words which I did not understand, but which she said after me, giving me the letter addressed to Selenis. I burnt the letter in the flame of the spirits, beneath the light of the moon, and the credulous lady told me she saw the characters she had traced ascending in the rays of the planet.

We then got into the bath, and the letter, which was written in silver characters on green paper appeared on the surface of the water in the course of ten minutes. As soon as Madame d'Urfe saw it, she picked it up reverently and got out of the bath with me.

We dried and scented ourselves, and proceeded to put on our clothes. As soon as we were in a state of decency I told Madame d'Urfe that she might read the epistle, which she had placed on a scented silk cushion. She obeyed, and I saw sadness visibly expressed on her features when she saw that her hypostasis was deferred till the arrival of Querilinthus, whom she would see with me at Marseilles in the spring of next year. The genius also said that the Countess Lascaris could not only do her harm, and that she should consult me as to the best means of getting rid of her. The letter ended by ordering her not to leave at Aix a lady who had lost her husband, and had a daughter who was destined to be of great service to the fraternity of the R. C. She was to take them to Alsace, and not to leave them till they were there, and safe from that danger which threatened them if they were left to themselves.

Madame d'Urfe, who with all her folly was an exceedingly benevolent woman, commended the widow to my care enthusiastically, and seemed impatient to hear her whole history. I told her all the circumstances which I thought would strengthen her in her resolution to befriend them, and promised to introduce the ladies to them at the first opportunity.

We returned to Aix, and spent the night in discussing the phantoms which coursed through her brain. All was going on well, and my only care was for the journey to Aix, and how to obtain the complete enjoyment of Mimi after having so well deserved her favours.

I had a run of luck at play the next day, and in the evening I gave Madame d'Ache an agreeable surprise by telling her that I should accompany her and her Mimi to Colmar. I told her that I should begin by introducing her to the lady whom I had the honour to accompany, and I begged her to be ready by the next day as the marchioness was impatient to see her. I could see that she could scarcely believe her ears, for she thought Madame d'Urfe was in love with me, and she could not understand her desire to make the acquaintance of two ladies who might be dangerous rivals.

I conducted them to Madame d'Urfe at the appointed hour, and they were received with a warmth which surprised them exceedingly, for they could not be expected to know that their recommendation came from the moon. We made a party of four, and while the two ladies talked together in the fashion of ladies who have seen the world, I paid Mimi a particular attention, which her mother understood very well, but which Madame d'Urfe attributed to the young lady's connection with the Rosy Cross.

In the evening we all went to a ball, and there the Corticelli, who was always trying to annoy me, danced as no young lady would dance. She executed rapid steps, pirouetted, cut capers, and shewed her legs; in short, she behaved like a ballet-girl. I was on thorns. An officer, who either ignored, or pretended to ignore, my supposed relation to her, asked me if she was a professional dancer. I heard another man behind me say that he thought he remembered seeing her on the boards at Prague. I resolved on hastening my departure, as I foresaw that if I stayed much longer at Aix the wretched girl would end by costing me my life.

As I have said, Madame d'Ache had a good society manner, and this put her in Madame d'Urfe's good graces, who saw in her politeness a new proof of the favour of Selenis. Madame d'Ache felt, I suppose, that she owed me some return after all I had done for her, and left the ball early, so that when I took Mimi home I found myself alone with her, and at perfect liberty to do what I liked. I profited by the opportunity, and remained with Mimi for two hours, finding her so complaisant and even passionate that when I left her I had nothing more to desire.

In three days time I provided the mother and daughter with their outfit, and we left Aix gladly in an elegant and convenient travelling carriage which I had provided. Half an hour before we left I made an acquaintance which afterwards proved fatal to me. A Flemish officer, unknown to me, accosted me, and painted his destitute condition in such sad colours that I felt obliged to give him twelve louis. Ten minutes after, he gave me a paper in which he acknowledged the debt, and named the time in which he could pay it. From the paper I ascertained that his name was Malingan. In ten months the reader will hear the results.

Just us we were starting I shewed the Corticelli a carriage with four places, in which she, her mother, and the two maids, were to travel. At this she trembled, her pride was wounded, and for a moment I thought she was going out of her mind; she rained sobs, abuse, and curses on me. I stood the storm unmoved, however, and Madame d'Urfe only laughed at her niece's paroxysms, and seemed delighted to find herself sitting opposite to me with the servant of Selenis beside her, while Mimi was highly pleased to be so close to me.

We got to Liege at nightfall on the next day, and I contrived to make Madame d'Urfe stay there the day following, wishing to get horses to take us through the Ardennes, and thus to have the charming Mimi longer in my possession.

I rose early and went out to see the town. By the great bridge, a woman, so wrapped up in a black mantilla that only the tip of her nose was visible, accosted me, and asked me to follow her into a house with an open door which she shewed me.

"As I have not the pleasure of knowing you," I replied, "prudence will not allow me to do so."

"You do know me, though," she replied, and taking me to the corner of a neighbouring street she shewed me her face. What was my surprise to see the fair Stuart of Avignon, the statue of the Fountain of Vaucluse. I was very glad to meet her.

In my curiosity I followed her into the house, to a room on the first floor, where she welcomed me most tenderly. It was all no good, for I felt angry with her, and despised her advances, no doubt, because I had Mimi, and wished to keep all my love for her. However, I took three louis out of my purse and gave them to her, asking her to tell me her history.

"Stuart," she said, "was only my keeper; my real name is Ranson, and I am the mistress of a rich landed proprietor. I got back to Liege after many sufferings."

"I am delighted to hear that you are more prosperous now, but it must be confessed that your behaviour at Avignon was both preposterous and absurd. But the subject is not worth discussing. Good day, madam."

I then returned to my hotel to write an account of what I had seen to   the Marquis Grimaldi.

The next day we left Liège, and were two days passing through the Ardennes. This is one of the strangest tracts in Europe: a vast forest, the traditions of which furnished Ariosto with some splendid passages.

There is no town in the forest, and though one is obliged to cross it to pass from one country to another, hardly any of the necessaries of life are to be found in it.

The enquirer will seek in vain for vices or virtues, or manners of any kind. The inhabitants are devoid of correct ideas, but have wild notions of their own on the power of men they style scholars. It is enough to be a doctor to enjoy the reputation of an astrologer and a wizard. Nevertheless the Ardennes have a large population, as I was assured that there were twelve hundred churches in the forest. The people are good-hearted and even pleasant, especially the young girls; but as a general rule the fair sex is by no means fair in those quarters. In this vast district watered by the Meuse is the town of Bouillon—a regular hole, but in my time it was the freest place in Europe. The Duke of Bouillon was so jealous of his rights that he preferred the exercise of his prerogatives to all the honours he might have enjoyed at the Court of France. We stayed a day at Metz, but did not call on anyone; and in three days we reached

Colmar, where we left Madame d'Ache, whose good graces I had completely won. Her family, in extremely comfortable circumstances, received the mother and daughter with great affection. Mimi wept bitterly when I left her, but I consoled her by saying that I would come back before long. Madame d'Urfe seemed not to mind leaving them, and I consoled myself easily enough. While congratulating myself on having made mother and daughter happy, I adored the secret paths and ways of Divine Providence.

On the following day we went to Sulzbach, where the Baron of Schaumburg, who knew Madame d'Urfe, gave us a warm welcome. I should have been sadly boared in this dull place if it had not been for gaming. Madame d'Urfe, finding herself in need of company, encouraged the Corticelli to hope to regain my good graces, and, consequently, her own. The wretched girl, seeing how easily I had defeated her projects, and to what a pass of humiliation I had brought her, had changed her part, and was now submissive enough. She flattered herself that she would regain the favour she had completely lost, and she thought the day was won when she saw that Madame d'Ache and her daughter stayed at Colmar. But what she had more at heart than either my friendship or Madame d'Urfe's was the jewel-casket; but she dared not ask for it, and her hopes of seeing it again were growing dim. By her pleasantries at table which made Madame d'Urfe laugh she succeeded in giving me a few amorous twinges; but still I did not allow my feelings to relax my severity, and she continued to sleep with her mother.

A week after our arrival at Sulzbach I left Madame d'Urfe with the Baron of Schaumburg, and I went to Colmar in the hope of good fortune. But I was disappointed, as the mother and daughter had both made arrangements for getting married.

A rich merchant, who had been in love with the mother eighteen years before, seeing her a widow and still pretty, felt his early flames revive, and offered his hand and was accepted. A young advocate found Mimi to his taste, and asked her in marriage. The mother and daughter, fearing the results of my affection, and finding it would be a good match, lost no time in giving their consent. I was entertained in the family, and supped in the midst of a numerous and choice assemblage; but seeing that I should only annoy the ladies and tire myself in waiting for some chance favour if I stayed, I bade them adieu and returned to Sulzbach the next morning. I found there a charming girl from Strasburg, named Salzmann, three or four gamesters who had come to drink the waters, and several ladies, to whom I shall introduce the reader in the ensuing chapter.

CHAPTER XVI

I Send The Corticelli to Turin—Helen is Initiated Into The Mysteries of Love I Go to Lyons—My Arrival at Turin

One of the ladies, Madame Saxe, was intended by nature to win the devotion of a man of feeling; and if she had not had a jealous officer in her train who never let her go out of his sight, and seemed to threaten anyone who aspired to please, she would probably have had plenty of admirers. This officer was fond of piquet, but the lady was always obliged to sit close beside him, which she seemed to do with pleasure.

In the afternoon I played with him, and continued doing so for five or six days. After that I could stand it no longer, as when he had won ten or twelve louis he invariably rose and left me to myself. His name was d'Entragues; he was a fine-looking man, though somewhat thin, and had a good share of wit and knowledge of the world.

We had not played together for two days, when one afternoon he asked if I would like to take my revenge.

"No, I think not," said I, "for we don't play on the same principle. I play for amusement's sake and you play to win money."

"What do you mean? Your words are offensive."

"I didn't mean them to be offensive, but as a matter of fact, each time we have played you have risen after a quarter of an hour."

"You ought to be obliged to me, as otherwise you would have lost heavily."

"Possibly; but I don't think so."

"I can prove it to you:"

"I accept the offer, but the first to leave the table must forfeit fifty Louis."

"I agree; but money down."

"I never play on credit."

I ordered a waiter to bring cards, and I went to fetch four or five rolls of a hundred Louis each. We began playing for five Louis the game, each player putting down the fifty Louis wagered.

We began to play at three, and at nine o'clock d'Entragues said we might take some supper.

"I am not hungry," I replied, "but you can go if you want me to put the hundred Louis in my pocket."

He laughed at this and went on playing, but this lacy fair scowled at me, though I did not care in the least for that. All the guests went to supper, and returned to keep us company till midnight, but at that hour we found ourselves alone. D'Entragues saw what kind of man he had got hold of and said never a word, while I only opened my lips to score; we played with the utmost coolness.

At six o'clock the ladies and gentlemen who were taking the waters began to assemble. We were applauded for our determination, in spite of our grim look. The Louis were on the table; I had lost a hundred, and yet the game was going in my favour.

At nine the fair Madame Saxe put in an appearance, and shortly after Madame d'Urfe came in with M. de Schaumburg. Both ladies advised us to take a cup of chocolate. D'Entragues was the first to consent, and thinking that I was almost done he said,—

"Let us agree that the first man who asks for food, who absents himself for more than a quarter of an hour, or who falls asleep in his chair, loses the bet."

"I will take you at your word," I replied, "and I adhere to all your conditions."

The chocolate came, we took it, and proceeded with our play. At noon we were summoned to dinner, but we both replied that we were not hungry. At four o'clock we allowed ourselves to be persuaded into taking some soup. When supper-time came and we were still playing, people began to think that the affair was getting serious, and Madame Saxe urged us to divide the wager. D'Entragues, who had won a hundred louis, would have gladly consented, but I would not give in, and M. de Schaumburg pronounced me within my rights. My adversary might have abandoned the stake and still found himself with a balance to the good, but avarice rather than pride prevented his doing so. I felt the loss myself, but what I cared chiefly about was the point of honour. I still looked fresh, while he resembled a disinterred corpse. As Madame Saxe urged me strongly to give way, I answered that I felt deeply grieved at not being able to satisfy such a charming woman, but that there was a question of honour in the case; and I was determined not to yield to my antagonist if I sat there till I fell dead to the ground.

I had two objects in speaking thus: I wanted to frighten him and to make him jealous of me. I felt certain that a man in a passion of jealousy would be quite confused, and I hoped his play would suffer accordingly, and that I should not have the mortification of losing a hundred louis to his superior play, though I won the fifty louis of the wager.

The fair Madame Saxe gave me a glance of contempt and left us, but Madame d'Urfe, who believed I was infallible, avenged me by saying to d'Entragues, in a tone of the profoundest conviction,—

"O Lord! I pity you, sir."

The company did not return after supper, and we were left alone to our play. We played on all the night, and I observed my antagonist's face as closely as the cards. He began to lose his composure, and made mistakes, his cards got mixed up, and his scoring was wild. I was hardly less done up than he; I felt myself growing weaker, and I hoped to see him fall to the ground every moment, as I began to be afraid of being beaten in spite of the superior strength of my constitution. I had won back my money by day-break, and I cavilled with him for being away for more than a quarter of an hour. This quarrel about nothing irritated him, and roused me up; the difference of our natures produced these different results, and my stratagem succeeded because it was impromptu, and could not have been foreseen. In the same way in war, sudden stratagems succeed.

At nine o'clock Madame Saxe came in, her lover was losing.

"Now, sir," she said to me, "you may fairly yield."

"Madam," said I, "in hope of pleasing you, I will gladly divide the stakes and rise from the table."

The tone of exaggerated gallantry with which I pronounced these words, put d'Entragues into a rage, and he answered sharply that he would not desist till one of us was dead.

With a glance at the lady which was meant to be lovelorn, but which must have been extremely languid in my exhausted state, I said,—

"You see, Madam, that I am not the more obstinate of the two."

A dish of soup was served to us, but d'Entragues, who was in the last stage of exhaustion, had no sooner swallowed the soup than he fell from his chair in a dead faint. He was soon taken up, and after I had given six louis to the marker who had been watching for forty-eight hours, I pocketed the gold, and went to the apothecary's where I took a mild emetic. Afterwards I went to bed and slept for a few hours, and at three o'clock I made an excellent dinner.

D'Entragues remained in his room till the next day. I expected a quarrel, but the night brings counsel, and I made a mistake. As soon as he saw me he ran up to me and embraced me, saying,—

"I made a silly bet, but you have given me a lesson which will last me all my days, and I am much obliged to you for it."

"I am delighted to hear it, provided that your health has not suffered."

"No, I am quite well, but we will play no more together."

"Well, I hope we shan't play against each other any more."

In the course of eight or ten days I took Madame d'Urfe and the pretended Lascaris to Bale. We put up at the inn of the famous Imhoff, who swindled us, but, all the same, the "Three Kings" is the best inn in the town. I think I have noted that noon at Bale is at eleven o'clock—an absurdity due to some historic event, which I had explained to me but have forgotten. The inhabitants are said to be subject to a kind of madness, of which they are cured by taking the waters of Sulzbach; but they 'get it again as soon as they return.

We should have stayed at Bale some time, if it had not been for an incident which made me hasten our departure. It was as follows:

My necessities had obliged me to forgive the Corticelli to a certain extent, and when I came home early I spent the night with her; but when I came home late, as often happened, I slept in my own room. The little hussy, in the latter case, slept also alone in a room next to her mother's, through whose chamber one had to pass to get to the daughter's.

One night I came in at one o'clock, and not feeling inclined to sleep, I took a candle and went in search of my charmer. I was rather surprised to find Signora Laura's door half open, and just as I was going in the old woman came forward and took me by the arm, begging me not to go into her daughter's room.

"Why?" said I.

"She has been very poorly all the evening, and she is in need of sleep."

"Very good; then I will sleep too."

So saying I pushed the mother to one side, and entering the girl's room I found her in bed with someone who was hiding under the sheets.

I gazed at the picture for a moment and then began to laugh, and sitting down on the bed begged to enquire the name of the happy individual whom I should have the pleasure of throwing out of the window. On a chair I saw the coat, trousers, hat, and cane of the gentleman; but as I had my two trusty pistols about me I knew I had nothing to fear; however, I did not want to make a noise.

With tears in her eyes, and trembling all over, the girl took my hand and begged me to forgive her.

"It's a young lord," said she, "and I don't even know his name."

"Oh, he is a young lord, is he? and you don't know his name, you little hussy, don't you? Well, he will tell me himself."

So saying, I took a pistol and vigorously stripped the sheets off the cuckoo who had got into my nest. I saw the face of a young man whom I did not know, his head covered with a nightcap, but the rest perfectly naked, as indeed was my mistress. He turned his back to me to get his shirt which he had thrown on the floor, but seizing him by the arm I held him firmly, with my pistol to his forehead.

"Kindly tell me your name, fair sir."

"I am Count B——, canon of Bale."

"And do you think you have been performing an ecclesiastical function here?"

"No sir, no, and I hope you will forgive me and the lady too, for I am the only guilty party."

"I am not asking you whether she is guilty or not."

"Sir, the countess is perfectly innocent."

I felt in a good temper, and far from being angry I was strongly inclined to laugh. I found the picture before me an attractive one; it was amusing and voluptuous. The sight of the two nudities on the bed was a truly lascivious one, and I remained contemplating it in silence for a quarter of an hour, occupied in resisting a strong temptation to take off my clothes and lie beside them. The only thing which prevented my yielding to it was the fear that I might find the canon to be a fool, incapable of playing the part with dignity. As for the Corticelli, she soon passed from tears to laughter, and would have done it well, but if, as I feared, the canon was a blockhead, I should have been degrading myself.

I felt certain that neither of them had guessed my thoughts, so I rose and told the canon to put on his clothes.

"No one must hear anything more of this," said I, "but you and I will go to a distance of two hundred paces and burn a little powder."

"No, no, sir," cried my gentleman, "you may take me where you like, and kill me if you please, but I was not meant for a fighting man."

"Really?"

"Yes, sir, and I only became a priest to escape the fatal duty of duelling."

"Then you are a coward, and will not object to a good thrashing?"

"Anything you like, but it would be cruelty, for my love blinded me. I only came here a quarter of an hour ago, and the countess and her governess were both asleep."

"You are a liar."

"I had only just taken off my shirt when you came, and I have never seen this angel before."

"And that's gospel truth," said the Corticelli.

"Are you aware that you are a couple of impudent scoundrels? And as for you, master canon, you deserve to be roasted like St. Laurence."

In the meanwhile the wretched ecclesiastic had huddled on his clothes.

"Follow me, sir," said I, in a tone which froze the marrow of his bones; and I accordingly took him to my room.

"What will you do," said I, "if I forgive you and let you go without putting you to shame?"

"I will leave in an hour and a half, and you shall never see me here again; but even if we meet in the future, you will find me always ready to do you a service."

"Very good. Begone, and in the future take more precautions in your amorous adventures."

After this I went to bed, well pleased with what I had seen and what I had done, for I now had complete power over the Corticelli.

In the morning I called on her as soon as I got up, and told her to pack up her things, forbidding her to leave her room till she got into the carriage.

"I shall say I am ill."

"Just as you please, but nobody will take any notice of you."

I did not wait for her to make any further objections, but proceeded to tell the tale of what had passed to Madame d'Urfe, slightly embroidering the narrative. She laughed heartily, and enquired of the oracle what must be done with the Lascaris after her evident pollution by the evil genius disguised as a priest. The oracle replied that we must set out the next day for Besancon, whence she would go to Lyons and await me there, while I would take the countess to Geneva, and thus send her back to her native country.

The worthy visionary was enchanted with this arrangement, and saw in it another proof of the benevolence of Selenis, who would thus give her an opportunity of seeing young Aranda once more. It was agreed that I was to rejoin her in the spring of the following year, to perform the great operation which was to make her be born a man. She had not the slightest doubts as to the reasonableness of this performance.

All was ready, and the next day we started; Madame d'Urfe and I in the travelling carriage, and the Corticelli, her mother, and the servants in another conveyance.

When we got to Besancon Madame d'Urfe left me, and on the next day I journeyed towards Geneva with the mother and daughter.

On the way I not only did not speak to my companions, I did not so much as look at them. I made them have their meals with a servant from the Franche Comte, whom I had taken on M. de Schaumburg's recommendation.

I went to my banker, and asked him to get me a good coachman, who would take two ladies of my acquaintance to Turin.

When I got back to the inn I wrote to the Chevalier Raiberti, sending him a bill of exchange. I warned him that in three or four days after the receipt of my letter he would be accosted by a Bolognese dancer and her mother, bearing a letter of commendation. I begged him to see that they lodged in a respectable house, and to pay for them on my behalf. I also said that I should be much obliged if he would contrive that she should dance, even for nothing, at the carnival, and I begged him to warn her that, if I heard any tales about her when I came to Turin, our relations would be at an end.

The following day a clerk of M. Tronchin's brought a coachman for me to see. The man said he was ready to start as soon as he had had his dinner.
I confirmed the agreement he had made with the banker, I summoned the two Corticellis, and said to the coachman,

"These are the persons you are to drive, and they will pay you when they reach Turin in safety with their luggage. You are to take four days and a half for the journey, as is stipulated in the agreement, of which they have one copy and you another." An hour after he called to put the luggage in.

The Corticelli burst into tears, but I was not so cruel as to send her away without any consolation. Her bad conduct had been severely enough punished already. I made her dine with me, and as I gave her the letter for M. Raiberti, and twenty-five Louis for the journey, I told her what I had written to the gentleman, who would

93

take good care of them. She asked me for a trunk containing three dresses and a superb mantle which Madame d'Urfe had given her before she became mad, but I said that we would talk of that at Turin. She dared not mention the casket, but continued weeping; however, she did not move me to pity. I left her much better off than when I first knew her; she had good clothes, good linen, jewels, and an exceedingly pretty watch I had given her; altogether a good deal more than she deserved.

As she was going I escorted her to the carriage, less for politeness' sake than to commend her once more to the coachman. When she was fairly gone I felt as if a load had been taken off my back, and I went to look up my worthy syndic, whom the reader will not have forgotten. I had not written to him since I was in Florence, and I anticipated the pleasure of seeing his surprise, which was extreme. But after gazing at me for a moment he threw his arms round my neck, kissed me several times, and said he had not expected the pleasure of seeing me.

"How are our sweethearts getting on?"

"Excellently. They are always talking about you and regretting your absence; they will go wild with joy when they know you are here."

"You must tell them directly, then."

"I will go and warn them that we shall all sup together this evening. By the way, M. de Voltaire has given up his house at Delices to M. de Villars, and has gone to live at Ferney."

"That makes no difference to me, as I was not thinking of calling on him this time. I shall be here for two or three weeks, and I mean to devote my time to you."

"You are too good."

"Will you give me writing materials before you go out? I will write a few letters while you are away."

He put me in possession of his desk, and I wrote to my late housekeeper, Madame Lebel, telling her that I was going to spend three weeks at Geneva, and that if I were sure of seeing her I would gladly pay a visit to Lausanne. Unfortunately, I also wrote to the bad Genoese poet, Ascanio Pogomas, or Giaccomo Passano, whom I had met at Leghorn. I told him to go to Turin and to wait for me there. At the same time I wrote to M. F——, to whom I had commended him, asking him to give the poet twelve Louis for the journey.

My evil genius made me think of this man, who was an imposing-looking fellow, and had all the air of a magician, to introduce him to Madame d'Urfe as a great adept. You will see, dear reader, in the course of a year whether I had reason to repent of this fatal inspiration.

As the syndic and I were on our way to our young friend's house I saw an elegant English carriage for sale, and I exchanged it for mine, giving the owner a hundred Louis as well. While the bargain was going on the uncle of the young theologian who argued so well, and to whom I had given such pleasant lessons in physiology, came up to me, embraced me, and asked me to dine with him the next day.

Before we got to the house the syndic informed me that we should find another extremely pretty but uninitiated girl present.

"All the better," said I, "I shall know how to regulate my conduct, and perhaps I may succeed in initiating her."

In my pocket I had placed a casket containing a dozen exquisite rings. I had long been aware that such trifling presents are often very serviceable.

The moment of meeting those charming girls once more was one of the happiest I have ever enjoyed. In their greeting I read delight and love of pleasure. Their love was without envy or jealousy, or any ideas which would have injured their self-esteem. They felt worthy of my regard, as they had lavished their favours on me without any degrading feelings, and drawn by the same emotion that had drawn me.

The presence of the neophyte obliged us to greet each other with what is called decency, and she allowed me to kiss her without raising her eyes, but blushing violently.

After the usual commonplaces had passed and we had indulged in some double meanings which made us laugh and her look thoughtful, I told her she was pretty as a little love, and that I felt sure that her mind, as beautiful as its casket, could harbour no prejudices.

"I have all the prejudices which honour and religion suggest," she modestly replied.

I saw that this was a case requiring very delicate treatment. There was no question of carrying the citadel by sudden assault. But, as usual, I fell in love with her.

The syndic having pronounced my name, she said,—

"Ah! then, you, sir, are the person who discussed some very singular questions with my cousin, the pastor's niece. I am delighted to make your acquaintance."

"I am equally pleased to make yours, but I hope the pastor's niece said nothing against me."

"Not at all; she has a very high opinion of you."

"I am going to dine with her to-morrow, and I shall take care to thank her."

"To-morrow! I should like to be there, for I enjoy philosophical discussions though I never dare to put a word in."

The syndic praised her discretion and wisdom in such a manner that I was convinced he was in love with her, and that he had either seduced her or was trying to do so. Her name was Helen. I asked the young ladies if Helen was their sister. The eldest replied, with a sly smile, that she was a sister, but as yet she had no brother; and with this explanation she ran up to Helen and kissed her. Then the syndic and I vied with each other in paying her compliments, telling her that we hoped to be her brothers. She blushed, but gave no answer to our gallantries. I then drew forth my casket, and seeing that all the girls were enchanted with the rings, I told them to choose which ones they liked best. The charming Helen imitated their example, and repaid me with a modest kiss. Soon after she left us, and we were once more free, as in old times.

The syndic had good cause to shew for his love of Helen. She was not merely pleasing, she was made to inspire a violent passion. However, the three friends had no hope of making her join in their pleasures, for they said that she had invincible feelings of modesty where men were concerned.

We supped merrily, and after supper we began our sports again, the syndic remaining as usual a mere looker-on, and well pleased with his part. I treated each of the three nymphs to two courses, deceiving them whenever I was forced by nature to do so. At midnight we broke up, and the worthy syndic escorted me to the door of my lodging.

The day following I went to the pastor's and found a numerous party assembled, amongst others M. d'Harcourt and M. de Ximenes, who told me that M. de Voltaire knew that I was at Geneva and hoped to see me. I replied by a profound bow. Mdlle. Hedvig, the pastor's niece, complimented me, but I was still better pleased to see her cousin Helen. The theologian of twenty-two was fair and pleasant to the eyes, but she had not that 'je ne sais quoi', that shade of bitter-sweet, which adds zest to hope as well as pleasure. However, the evident friendship between Hedvig and Helen gave me good hopes of success with the latter.

We had an excellent dinner, and while it lasted the conversation was restricted to ordinary topics; but at dessert the pastor begged M. de Ximenes to ask his niece some questions. Knowing his worldwide reputation, I expected him to put her some problem in geometry, but he only asked whether a lie could be justified on the principle of a mental reservation.

Hedvig replied that there are cases in which a lie is necessary, but that the principle of a mental reservation is always a cheat.

"Then how could Christ have said that the time in which the world was to come to an end was unknown to Him?"

"He was speaking the truth; it was not known to Him."

"Then he was not God?"

"That is a false deduction, for since God may do all things, He may certainly be ignorant of an event in futurity."

I thought the way in which she brought in the word "futurity" almost sublime. Hedvig was loudly applauded, and her uncle went all round the table to kiss her. I had a very natural objection on the tip of my tongue, which she might have found difficult to answer, but I wanted to get into her good graces and I kept my own counsel.

M. d'Harcourt was urged to ask her some questions, but he replied in the words of Horace, 'Nulla mihi religio est'. Then Hedvig turned to me and asked me to put her some hard question, "something difficult, which you don't know yourself."

"I shall be delighted. Do you grant that a god possesses in a supreme degree the qualities of man?"

"Yes, excepting man's weaknesses."

"Do you class the generative power as a weakness?"

"No."

"Will you tell me, then, of what nature would have been the offspring of a union between a god and a mortal woman?"

Hedvig looked as red as fire.

The pastor and the other guests looked at each other, while I gazed fixedly at the young theologian, who was reflecting. M. d'Harcourt said that we should have to send for Voltaire to settle a question so difficult, but as Hedvig had collected her thoughts and seemed ready to speak everybody was silent.

"It would be absurd," said she, "to suppose that a deity could perform such an action without its having any results. At the end of nine months a woman would be delivered a male child, which would be three parts man and one part god."

At these words all the guests applauded, M. de Ximenes expressed his admiration of the way the question had been solved, adding,—

"Naturally, if the son of the woman married, his children would be seven-eighths men and one-eighth gods."

"Yes," said I, "unless he married a goddess, which would have made the proportion different."

"Tell me exactly," said Hedvig, "what proportion of divinity there would be in a child of the sixteenth generation."

"Give me a pencil and I will soon tell you," said M. de Ximenes.

"There is no need to calculate it," said I; "the child would have some small share of the wit which you enjoy."

Everybody applauded this gallant speech, which did not by any means offend the lady to whom it was addressed.

This pretty blonde was chiefly desirable for the charms of her intellect. We rose from the table and made a circle round her, but she told us with much grace not to pay her any more compliments.

I took Helen aside, and told her to get her cousin to choose a ring from my casket, which I gave her, and she seemed glad to execute the commission. A quarter of an hour afterwards Hedvig came to shew me her hand adorned with the ring she had chosen. I kissed it rapturously, and she must have guessed from the warmth of my kisses with what feelings she had inspired me.

In the evening Helen told the syndic and the three girls all about the morning's discussion without leaving out the smallest detail. She told the story with ease and grace, and I had no occasion to prompt her. We begged her to stay to supper, but she whispered something to the three friends, and they agreed that it was impossible; but she said that she might spend a couple of days with them in their country house on the lake, if they would ask her mother.

At the syndic's request the girls called on the mother the next day, and the day after that they went off with Helen. The same evening we went and supped with them, but we could not sleep there. The syndic was to take me to a house at a short distance off, where we should be very comfortable. This being the case there was no hurry, and the eldest girl said that the syndic and I could leave whenever we liked, but that they were going to bed. So saying she took Helen to her room, while the two others slept in another room. Soon after the syndic went into the room where Helen was, and I visited the two others.

I had scarcely been with my two sweethearts for an hour when the syndic interrupted my erotic exploits by begging me to go.

"What have you done with Helen?" I asked.

"Nothing; she's a simpleton, and an intractable one. She hid under the sheets and would not look at my performance with her friend."

"You ought to go to her direct."

"I have done so, but she repulsed me again and again. I have given it up, and shall not try it again, unless you will tame her for me."

"How is it to be done?"

"Come to dinner to-morrow. I shall be away at Geneva. I shall be back by supper-time. I wish we could give her too much to drink!"

"That would be a pity. Let me see what I can do."

I accordingly went to dine with them by myself the next day, and they entertained me in all the force of the word. After dinner we went for a walk, and the three friends understanding my aims left me alone with the intractable girl, who resisted my caresses in a manner which almost made me give up the hope of taming her.

"The syndic," said I, "is in love with you, and last night . . .

"Last night," she said, "he amused himself with his old friend. I am for everyone's following their own tastes, but I expect to be allowed to follow mine."

"If I could gain your heart I should be happy."

"Why don't you invite the pastor and my cousin to dine with you? I could come too, for the pastor makes much of everyone who loves his niece."

"I am glad to hear that. Has she a lover?"

"No."

"I can scarcely believe it. She is young, pretty, agreeable, and very clever."

"You don't understand Genevan ways. It is because she is so clever that no young man falls in love with her. Those who might be attracted by her personal charms hold themselves aloof on account of her intellectual capacities, as they would have to sit in silence before her."

"Are the young Genevans so ignorant, then?"

"As a rule they are. Some of them have received excellent educations, but in a general way they are full of prejudice. Nobody wishes to be considered a fool or a blockhead, but clever women are not appreciated; and if a girl is witty or well educated she endeavors to hide her lights, at least if she desires to be married."

"Ah! now I see why you did not open your lips during our discussion."

"No, I know I have nothing to hide. This was not the motive which made me keep silence, but the pleasure of listening. I admired my cousin, who was not afraid to display her learning on a subject which any other girl would have affected to know nothing about."

"Yes, affected, though she might very probably know as much as her grandmother."

"That's a matter of morals, or rather of prejudices."

"Your reasoning is admirable, and I am already longing for the party you so cleverly suggested."

"You will have the pleasure of being with my cousin."

"I do her justice. Hedvig is certainly a very interesting and agreeable girl, but believe me it is your presence that will constitute my chief enjoyment."

"And how if I do not believe you?"

"You would wrong me and give me pain, for I love you dearly."

"In spite of that you have deceived me. I am sure that you have given marks of your affection to those three young ladies. For my part I pity them."

"Why?"

"Because neither of them can flatter herself that you love her, and her alone."

"And do you think that your delicacy of feeling makes you happier than they are?"

"Yes, I think so though of course, I have no experience in the matter. Tell me truly, do you think I am right?"

"Yes, I do."

"I am delighted to hear it; but you must confess that to associate me with them in your attentions would not be giving me the greatest possible proof of your love."

"Yes, I do confess it, and I beg your pardon. But tell me how I should set to work to ask the pastor to dinner."

"There will be no difficulty. Just call on him and ask him to come, and if you wish me to be of the party beg him to ask my mother and myself."

"Why your mother?"

"Because he has been in love with her these twenty years, and loves her still."

"And where shall I give this dinner?"

"Is not M. Tronchin your banker?"

"Yes."

"He has a nice pleasure house on the lake; ask him to lend it you for the day; he will be delighted to do so. But don't tell the syndic or his three friends anything about it; they can hear of it afterwards."

"But do you think your learned cousin will be glad to be in my company?"

"More than glad, you may be sure."

"Very good, everything will be arranged by tomorrow. The day after, you will be returning to Geneva, and the party will take place two or three days later."

The syndic came back in due course, and we had a very pleasant evening. After supper the ladies went to bed as before, and I went with the eldest girl while the syndic visited the two younger ones. I knew that it would be of no use to try to do anything with Helen, so I contented myself with a few kisses, after which I wished them good night and passed on to the next room. I found them in a deep sleep, and the syndic seemed visibly bored. He did not look more cheerful when I told him that I had had no success with Helen.

"I see," said he, "that I shall waste my time with the little fool. I think I shall give her up."

"I think that's the best thing you could do," I replied, "for a man who languishes after a woman who is either devoid of feeling or full of caprice, makes himself her dupe. Bliss should be neither too easy nor too hard to be won."

The next day we returned to Geneva, and M. Tronchin seemed delighted to oblige me. The pastor accepted my invitation, and said I was sure to be charmed with Helen's mother. It was easy to see that the worthy man cherished a tenderness for her, and if she responded at all it would be all the better for my purposes.

I was thinking of supping with the charming Helen and her three friends at the house on the lake, but an express summoned me to Lausanne. Madame Lebel, my old housekeeper, invited me to sup with her and her husband. She wrote that she had made her husband promise to take her to Lausanne as soon as she got my letter, and she added she was sure that I would resign everything to give her the pleasure of seeing me. She notified the hour at which she would be at her mother's house.

Madame Lebel was one of the ten or twelve women for whom in my happy youth I cherished the greatest affection. She had all the qualities to make a man a good wife, if it had been my fate to experience such felicity. But perhaps I did well not to tie myself down with irrevocable bonds, though now my independence is another name for slavery. But if I had married a woman of tact, who would have ruled me unawares to myself, I should have taken care of my fortune and have had children, instead of being lonely and penniless in my old age.

But I must indulge no longer in digressions on the past which cannot be recalled, and since my recollections make me happy I should be foolish to cherish idle regrets.

I calculated that if I started directly I should get to Lausanne an hour before Madame Lebel, and I did not hesitate to give her this proof of my regard. I must here warn my readers, that, though I loved this woman well, I was then occupied with another passion, and no voluptuous thought mingled with my desire of seeing her. My esteem for her was enough to hold my passions in check, but I esteemed Lebel too, and nothing would have induced me to disturb the happiness of this married pair.

I wrote in haste to the syndic, telling him that an important and sudden call obliged me to start for Lausanne, but that I should have the pleasure of supping with him and his three friends at Geneva on the following day.

I knocked at Madame Dubois's door at five o'clock, almost dying with hunger. Her surprise was extreme, for she did not know that her daughter was going to meet me at her house. Without more ado I gave her two louis to get us a good supper.

At seven o'clock, Madame Lebel, her husband, and a child of eighteen months, whom I easily recognized as my own, arrived. Our meeting was a happy one indeed; we spent ten hours at table, and mirth and joy prevailed. At day-break she started for Soleure, where Lebel had business. M. de Chavigni had desired to be remembered most affectionately to me. Lebel assured me that the ambassador was extremely kind to his wife, and he thanked me heartily for having given such a woman up to him. I could easily see that he was a happy husband, and that his wife was as happy as he.

My dear housekeeper talked to me about my son. She said that nobody suspected the truth, but that neither she nor Lebel (who had faithfully kept his promise, and had not consummated the marriage for the two months agreed upon) had any doubts.

"The secret," said Lebel to me, "will never be known, and your son will be my sole heir, or will share my property with my children if I ever have any, which I doubt."

"My dear," said his wife, "there is somebody who has very strong suspicions on the subject, and these suspicions will gain strength as the child grows older; but we have nothing to fear on that score, as she is well paid to keep the secret."

"And who is this person?" said I.

"Madame——. She has not forgotten the past, and often speaks of you."

"Will you kindly remember me to her?"

"I shall be delighted to do so, and I am sure the message will give her great pleasure."

Lebel shewed me my ring, and I shewed him his, and gave him a superb watch for my son.

"You must give it him," I said, "when you think he is old enough."

We shall hear of the young gentleman in twenty-one years at Fontainebleau.

I passed three hours in telling them of all the adventures I had during the twenty-seven months since we had seen one another. As to their history, it was soon told; it had all the calm which belongs to happiness.

Madame Lebel was as pretty as ever, and I could see no change in her, but I was no longer the same man. She thought me less lively than of old, and she was right. The Renaud had blasted me, and the pretended Lascaris had given me a great deal of trouble and anxiety.

We embraced each other tenderly, and the wedded pair returned to Soleure and I to Geneva; but feeling that I wanted rest I wrote to the syndic that I was not well and could not come till the next day, and after I had done so I went to bed.

The next day, the eve of my dinner party, I ordered a repast in which no expense was to be spared. I did not forget to tell the landlord to get me the best wines, the choicest liqueurs, ices, and all the materials for a bowl of punch. I told him that we should be six in number, for I foresaw that M. Tronchin would dine with us. I was right; I found him at his pretty house ready to receive us, and I had not much trouble in inducing him to stay. In the evening I thought it as well to tell the syndic and his three friends about it in Helen's presence, while she, feigning ignorance, said that her mother had told her they were going somewhere or other to dinner.

"I am delighted to hear it," said I; "it must be at M. Tronchin's."

My dinner would have satisfied the most exacting gourmet, but Hedvig was its real charm. She treated difficult theological questions with so much grace, and rationalised so skilfully, that though one might not be convinced it was impossible to help being attracted. I have never seen any theologian who could treat the most difficult points with so much facility, eloquence, and real dignity, and at dinner she completed her conquest of myself. M. Tronchin, who had never heard her speak before, thanked me a hundred times for having procured him this pleasure, and being obliged to leave us by the call of business he asked us to meet again in two days' time.

I was much interested during the dessert by the evident tenderness of the pastor for Helen's mother. His amorous eloquence grew in strength as he irrigated his throat with champagne, Greek wine, and eastern liqueurs. The lady seemed pleased, and was a match for him as far as drinking was concerned, while the two girls and myself only drank with sobriety. However, the mixture of wines, and above all the punch, had done their work, and my charmers were slightly elevated. Their spirits were delightful, but rather pronounced.

I took this favourable opportunity to ask the two aged lovers if I might take the young ladies for a walk in the garden by the lake, and they told us enthusiastically to go and enjoy ourselves. We went out arm in arm, and in a few minutes we were out of sight of everyone.

"Do you know," said I to Hedvig, "that you have made a conquest of   M. Tronchin?"

"Have I? The worthy banker asked me some very silly questions."

"You must not expect everyone to be able to contend with you."

"I can't help telling you that your question pleased me best of all. A bigoted theologian at the end of the table seemed scandalized at the question and still more at the answer."

"And why?"

"He says I ought to have told you that a deity could not impregnate a woman. He said that he would explain the reason to me if I were a man, but being a woman and a maid he could not with propriety expound such mysteries. I wish you would tell me what the fool meant."

"I should be very glad, but you must allow me to speak plainly, and I shall have to take for granted that you are acquainted with the physical conformation of a man."

"Yes, speak as plainly as you like, for there is nobody to hear what we say; but I must confess that I am only acquainted with the peculiarities of the male by theory and reading. I have no practical knowledge. I have seen statues, but I have never seen or examined a real live man. Have you, Helen?"

"I have never wished to do so."

"Why not? It is good to know everything."

"Well, Hedvig, your theologian meant to say that a god was not capable of this."

"What is that?"

"Give me your hand."

"I can feel it, and have thought it would be something like that; without this provision of nature man would not be able to fecundate his mate. And how could the foolish theologian maintain that this was an imperfection?"

"Because it is the result of desire, Hedvig, and it would not have taken place in me if I had not been charmed with you, and if I had not conceived the most seducing ideas of the beauties that I cannot see from the view of the beauties I can see. Tell me frankly whether feeling that did not give you an agreeable sensation."

"It did, and just in the place where your hand is now. Don't you feel a pleasant tickling there, Helen, after what the gentleman has been saying to us?"

"Yes, I feel it, but I often do, without anything to excite me."

"And then," said I, "nature makes you appease it . . . thus?"

"Not at all."

"Oh, yes!" said Hedvig. "Even when we are asleep our hands seek that spot as if by instinct, and if it were not for that solace I think we should get terribly ill."

As this philosophical discourse, conducted by the young theologian in quite a professional manner, proceeded, we reached a beautiful basin of water, with a flight of marble steps for bathers. Although the air was cool our heads were hot, and I conceived the idea of telling them that it would do them good to bathe their feet, and that if they would allow me I would take off their shoes and stockings.

"I should like to so much," said Hedvig.

"And I too," said Helen.

"Then sit down, ladies, on the first step."

They proceeded to sit down and I began to take off their shoes, praising the beauty of their legs, and pretending for the present not to want to go farther than the knee. When they got into the water they were obliged to pick up their clothes, and I encouraged them to do so.

"Well, well," said Hedvig, "men have thighs too."

Helen, who would have been ashamed to be beaten by her cousin, was not backward in shewing her legs.

"That will do, charming maids," said I, "you might catch cold if you stayed longer in the water."

They walked up backwards, still holding up their clothes for fear of wetting them, and it was then my duty to wipe them dry with all the handkerchiefs I had. This pleasant task left me at freedom to touch and see, and the reader will imagine that I did my best in that direction. The fair theologian told me I wanted to know too much, but Helen let me do what I liked with such a tender and affectionate expression that it was as much as I could do to keep within bounds. At last, when I had drawn on their shoes and stockings, I told them that I was delighted to have seen the hidden charms of the two prettiest girls in Geneva.

"What effect had it on you?" asked Hedvig.

"I daren't tell you to look, but feel, both of you."

"Do you bathe, too."

"It's out of the question, a man's undressing takes so much trouble."

"But we have still two hours before us, in which we need not fear any interruption."

This reply gave me a foretaste of the bliss I had to gain, but I did not wish to expose myself to an illness by going into the water in my present state. I noticed a summer-house at a little distance, and feeling sure that M. Tronchin had left the door open, I took the two girls on my arm and led them there without giving them any hint of my intentions. The summer-house was scented with vases of pot-pourri and adorned with engravings; but, best of all, there was a large couch which seemed made for repose and pleasure. I sat down on it between my two sweethearts, and as I caressed them I told them I was going to shew them something they had never seen before, and without more ado I displayed to their gaze the principal agent in the preservation of the human race. They got up to admire it, and taking a hand of each one I procured them some enjoyment, but in the middle of their labours an abundant flow of liquid threw them into the greatest astonishment.

"That," said I, "is the Word which makes men."

"It's beautiful!" cried Helen, laughing at the term "word."

"I have a word too," said Hedvig, "and I will shew it to you if you will wait a minute."

"Come, Hedvig, and I will save you the trouble of making it yourself, and will do it better."

"I daresay, but I have never done it with a man."

"No more have I," said Helen.

Placing them in front of me I gave them another ecstacy. We then sat down, and while I felt all their charms I let them touch me as much as they liked till I watered their hands a second time.

We made ourselves decent once more, and spent half an hour in kisses and caresses, and I then told them that they had made me happy only in part, but that I hoped they would make my bliss complete by presenting me with their maidenheads. I shewed them the little safety-bags invented by the English in the interests of the fair sex. They admired them greatly when I explained their use, and the fair theologian remarked to her cousin that she would think it over. We were now close friends, and soon promised to be something more; and we walked back and found the pastor and Helen's mother strolling by the side of the lake.

When I got back to Geneva I went to spend the evening with the three friends, but I took good care not to tell the syndic anything about my victory with Helen. It would only have served to renew his hopes, and he would have had this trouble for nothing. Even I would have done no good without the young theologian; but as Helen admired her she did not like to appear her inferior by refusing to imitate her freedom.

I did not see Helen that evening, but I saw her the next day at her mother's house, for I was in mere politeness bound to thank the old lady for the honour she had done me. She gave me a most friendly reception, and introduced me to two very pretty girls who were boarding with her. They might have interested me if I had been stopping long in Geneva, but as if was Helen claimed all my attraction.

"To-morrow," said the charming girl, "I shall be able to get a word with you at Madame Tronchin's dinner, and I expect Hedvig will have hit on some way for you to satisfy your desires."

The banker gave us an excellent dinner. He proudly told me that no inn-keeper could give such a good dinner as a rich gentleman who has a good cook, a good cellar, good silver plate, and china of the best quality. We were twenty of us at table, and the feast was given chiefly in honour of the learned theologian and myself, as a rich foreigner who spent money freely. M. de Ximenes, who had just arrived from Ferney was there, and told me that M. de Voltaire was expecting me, but I had foolishly determined not to go.

Hedvig shone in solving the questions put to her by the company. M. de Ximenes begged her to justify as best she could our first mother, who had deceived her husband by giving him the fatal apple to eat.

"Eve," she said, "did not deceive her husband, she only cajoled him into eating it in the hope of giving him one more perfection. Besides Eve had not been forbidden to eat the fruit by God, but only by Adam, and in all probability her woman's sense prevented her regarding the prohibition as serious."

At this reply, which I found full of sense and wit, two scholars from Geneva and even Hedvig's uncle began to murmur and shake their heads. Madame Tronchin said gravely that Eve had received the prohibition from God himself, but the girl only answered by a humble "I beg your pardon, madam." At this she turned to the pastor with a frightened manner, and said,—

"What do you say to this?"

"Madam, my niece is not infallible."

"Excuse me, dear uncle, I am as infallible as Holy Writ when I speak according to it."

"Bring a Bible, and let me see."

"Hedvig, my dear Hedvig, you are right after all. Here it is. The prohibition was given before woman was made."

Everybody applauded, but Hedvig remained quite calm; it was only the two scholars and Madame Tronchin who still seemed disturbed. Another lady then asked her if it was allowable to believe the history of the apple to be symbolical. She replied,—

"I do not think so, because it could only be a symbol of sexual union, and it is clear that such did not take place between Adam and Eve in the Garden of Eden."

"The learned differ on this point."

"All the worse for them, madam, the Scripture is plain enough. In the first verse of the fourth chapter it is written, that Adam knew his wife after they had been driven from the Garden, and that in consequence she conceived Cain."

"Yes, but the verse does not say that Adam did not know her before and consequently he might have done so."

"I cannot admit the inference, as in that case she would have conceived; for it would be absurd to suppose that two creatures who had just left God's hands, and were consequently as nearly perfect as is possible, could perform the act of generation without its having any result."

This reply gained everyone's applause, and compliments to Hedvig made the round of the table.

Mr. Tronchin asked her if the doctrine of the immortality of the soul could be gathered from the Old Testament alone.

"The Old Testament," she replied, "does not teach this doctrine; but, nevertheless, human reason teaches it, as the soul is a substance, and the destruction of any substance is an unthinkable proposition."

"Then I will ask you," said the banker, "if the existence of the soul is established in the Bible."

"Where there is smoke there is always fire."

"Tell me, then, if matter can think."

"I cannot answer that question, for it is beyond my knowledge. I can only say that as I believe God to be all powerful, I cannot deny Him the power to make matter capable of thought."

"But what is your own opinion?"

"I believe that I have a soul endowed with thinking capacities, but I do not know whether I shall remember that I had the honour of dining with you to-day after I die."

"Then you think that the soul and the memory may be separable; but in that case you would not be a theologian."

"One may be a theologian and a philosopher, for philosophy never contradicts any truth, and besides, to say 'I do not know' is not the same as 'I am sure'."

Three parts of the guests burst into cries of admiration, and the fair philosopher enjoyed seeing me laugh for pleasure at the applause. The pastor wept for joy, and whispered something to Helen's mother. All at once he turned to me, saying,—

"Ask my niece some question."

"Yes," said Hedvig, "but it must be something quite new."

"That is a hard task," I replied, "for how am I to know that what I ask is new to you? However, tell me if one must stop at the first principle of a thing one wants to understand."

"Certainly, and the reason is that in God there is no first principle, and He is therefore incomprehensible."

"God be praised! that is how I would have you answer. Can God have any self-consciousness?"

"There my learning is baffled. I know not what to reply. You should not ask me so hard a thing as that."

"But you wished for something new. I thought the newest thing would be to see you at a loss."

"That's prettily said. Be kind enough to reply for me, gentlemen, and teach me what to say."

Everybody tried to answer, but nothing was said worthy of record. Hedvig at last said,—

"My opinion is that since God knows all, He knows of His own existence, but you must not ask me how He knows it."

"That's well said," I answered; and nobody could throw any further light on the matter.

All the company looked on me as a polite Atheist, so superficial is the judgment of society, but it did not matter to me whether they thought me an Atheist or not.

M. de Ximenes asked Hedvig if matter had been created.

"I cannot recognize the word 'created,'" she replied. "Ask me whether matter was formed, and I shall reply in the affirmative. The word 'created' cannot have existence, for the existence of anything must be prior to the word which explains it."

"Then what meaning do you assign to the word 'created'?"

"Made out of nothing. You see the absurdity, for nothing must have first existed. I am glad to see you laugh. Do you think that nothingness could be created?"

"You are right."

"Not at all, not at all," said one of the guests, superciliously.

"Kindly tell me who was your teacher?" said M. de Ximenes.

"My uncle there."

"Not at all, my dear niece. I certainly never taught you what you have been telling us to-day. But my niece, gentlemen, reads and reflects over what she has read, perhaps with rather too much freedom, but I love her all the same, because she always ends by acknowledging that she knows nothing."

A lady who had not opened her lips hitherto asked Hedvig for a definition of spirit.

"Your question is a purely philosophical one, and I must answer that I do not know enough of spirit or matter to be able to give a satisfactory definition."

"But since you acknowledge the existence of Deity and must therefore have an abstract idea of spirit, you must have some notions on the subject, and should be able to tell me how it acts on matter."

"No solid foundation can be built on abstract ideas. Hobbes calls such ideas mere fantasms. One may have them, but if one begins to reason on them, one is landed in contradiction. I know that God sees me, but I should labour in vain if I endeavoured to prove it by reasoning, for reason tells us no one can see anything without organs of sight; and God being a pure spirit, and therefore without organs, it is scientifically impossible that He can see us any more than we can see Him. But Moses and several others have seen Him, and I believe it so, without attempting to reason on it."

"You are quite right," said I, "for you would be confronted by blank impossibility. But if you take to reading Hobbes you are in danger of becoming an Atheist."

"I am not afraid of that. I cannot conceive the possibility of Atheism."

After dinner everybody crowded round this truly astonishing girl, so that I had no opportunity of whispering my love. However, I went apart with Helen, who told me that the pastor and his niece were going to sup with her mother the following day.

"Hedvig," she added, "will stay the night and sleep with me as she always does when she comes to supper with her uncle. It remains to be seen if you are willing to hide in a place I will shew you at eleven o'clock tomorrow, in order to sleep with us. Call on my mother at that hour to-morrow, and I will find an opportunity of shewing you where it is. You will be safe though not comfortable, and if you grow weary you can console yourself by thinking that you are in our minds."

"Shall I have to stay there long?"

"Four hours at the most. At seven o'clock the street door is shut, and only opened to anyone who rings."

"If I happen to cough while I am in hiding might I be heard?"

"Yes, that might happen."

"There's a great hazard. All the rest is of no consequence; but no matter, I will risk all for the sake of so great happiness."

In the morning I paid the mother a visit, and as Helen was escorting me out she shewed me a door between the two stairs.

"At seven o'clock," said she, "the door will be open, and when you are in put on the bolt. Take care that no one sees you as you are entering the house."

At a quarter to seven I was already a prisoner. I found a seat in my cell, otherwise I should neither have been able to lie down or to stand up. It was a regular hole, and I knew by my sense of smell that hams and cheeses were usually kept there; but it contained none at present, for I fell all round to see how the land lay. As I was cautiously stepping round I felt my foot encounter some resistance, and putting down my hand I recognized the feel of linen. It was a napkin containing two plates, a nice roast fowl, bread, and a second napkin. Searching again I came across a bottle and a glass. I was grateful to my charmers for having thought of my stomach, but as I had purposely made a late and heavy meal I determined to defer the consumption of my cold collation till a later hour.

At nine o'clock I began, and as I had neither a knife nor a corkscrew I was obliged to break the neck of the bottle with a brick which I was fortunately able to detach from the mouldering floor. The wine was delicious old Neuchatel, and the fowl was stuffed with truffles, and I felt convinced that my two nymphs must have some rudimentary ideas on the subject of stimulants. I should have passed the time pleasantly enough if it had not been for the occasional visits of a rat, who nearly made me sick with his disgusting oduur. I remembered that I had been annoyed in the same way at Cologne under somewhat similar circumstances.

At last ten o'clock struck, and I heard the pastor's voice as he came downstairs talking; he warned the girls not to play any tricks together, and to go to sleep quietly. That brought back to my memory M. Rose leaving Madame Orio's house at Venice twenty-two years before; and reflecting on my character I found myself much changed, though not more reasonable; but if I was not so sensible to the charms of the sex, the two beauties who were awaiting me were much superior to Madame Orio's nieces.

In my long and profligate career in which I have turned the heads of some hundreds of ladies, I have become familiar with all the methods of seduction; but my guiding principle has been never to direct my attack against novices or those whose prejudices were likely to prove an obstacle except in the presence of another woman. I soon found out that timidity makes a girl averse to being seduced, while in company with another girl she is easily conquered; the weakness of the one brings on the fall of the other. Fathers and mothers are of the contrary opinion, but they are in the wrong. They will not trust their daughter to take a walk or go to a ball with a young man, but if she has another girl with her there is no difficulty made. I repeat, they are in the wrong; if the young man has the requisite skill their daughter is a lost woman. A feeling of false shame hinders them from making an absolute and determined resistance, and the first step once taken the rest comes inevitably and quickly. The girl grants some small favour, and immediately makes her friend grant a much greater one to hide her own blushes; and if the seducer is clever at his trade the young innocent will soon have gone too far to be able to draw back. Besides the more innocence a girl has, the less she knows of the methods of seduction. Before she has had time to think, pleasure attracts her, curiosity draws her a little farther, and opportunity does the rest.

For example, I might possibly have been able to seduce Hedvig without Helen, but I am certain I should never have succeeded with Helen if she had not seen her cousin take liberties with me which she no doubt thought contrary to the feelings of modesty which a respectable young woman ought to have.

Though I do not repent of my amorous exploits, I am far from wishing that my example should serve for the perversion of the fair sex, who have so many claims on my homage. I desire that what I say may be a warning to fathers and mothers, and secure me a place in their esteem at any rate.

Soon after the pastor had gone I heard three light knocks on my prison door. I opened it, and my hand was folded in a palm as soft as satin. All my being was moved. It was Helen's hand, and that happy moment had already repaid me for my long waiting.

"Follow me on tiptoe," she whispered, as soon as she had shut the door; but in my impatience I clasped her in my arms, and made her feel the effect which her mere presence had produced on me, while at the same time I assured myself of her docility. "There," she said, "now come upstairs softly after me."

I followed her as best I could in the darkness, and she took me along a gallery into a dark room, and then into a lighted one which contained Hedvig almost in a state of nudity. She came to me with open arms as soon as she saw me, and, embracing me ardently, expressed her gratitude for my long and dreary imprisonment.

"Divine Hedvig," I answered, "if I had not loved you madly I would not have stayed a quarter of an hour in that dismal cell, but I am ready to spend four hours there every day till I leave Geneva for your sake. But we must not lose any time; let us go to bed."

"Do you two go to bed," said Helen; "I will sleep on the sofa."

"No, no," cried Hedvig, "don't think of it; our fate must be exactly equal."

"Yes, darling Helen," said I, embracing her; "I love you both with equal ardour, and these ceremonies are only wasting the time in which I ought to be assuring you of my passion. Imitate my proceedings. I am going to undress, and then I shall lie in the middle of the bed. Come and lie beside me, and I'll shew you how I love you. If all is safe I will remain with you till you send me away, but whatever you do do not put out the light."

In the twinkling of an eye, discussing the theory of shame the while with the theological Hedvig, I presented myself to their gaze in the costume of Adam. Hedvig blushed and parted with the last shred of her modesty, citing the opinion of St. Clement Alexandrinus that the seat of shame is in the shirt. I praised the charming perfection of her shape, in the hope of encouraging Helen, who was slowly undressing herself; but an accusation of mock modesty from her cousin had more effect than all my praises. At last this Venus stood before me in a state of nature, covering her most secret parts with her hand, and hiding one breast with the other, and appearing woefully ashamed of what she could not conceal. Her modest confusion, this strife between departing modesty and rising passion, enchanted me.

Hedvig was taller than Helen; her skin was whiter, and her breasts double the size of Helen's; but in Helen there was more animation, her shape was more gently moulded, and her breast might have been the model for the Venus de Medicis.

She got bolder by degrees, and we spent some moments in admiring each other, and then we went to bed. Nature spoke out loudly, and all we wanted was to satisfy its demands. With much coolness I made a woman of Hedvig, and when all was over she kissed me and said that the pain was nothing in comparison with the pleasure.

The turn of Helen (who was six years younger than Hedvig) now came, but the finest fleece that I have ever seen was not won without difficulty. She was jealous of her cousin's success, and held it open with her two hands; and though she had to submit to great pain before being initiated into the amorous mysteries, her sighs were sighs of happiness, as she responded to my ardent efforts. Her great charms and the vivacity of her movements shortened the sacrifice, and when I left the sanctuary my two sweethearts saw that I needed repose.

The alter was purified of the blood of the victims, and we all washed, delighted to serve one another.

Life returned to me under their curious fingers, and the sight filled them with joy. I told them that I wished to enjoy them every night till I left Geneva, but they told me sadly that this was impossible.

"In five or six days time, perhaps, the opportunity may recur again, but that will be all."

"Ask us to sup at your inn to-morrow," said Hedvig; "and maybe, chance will favour the commission of a sweet felony."

I followed this advice.

I overwhelmed them with happiness for several hours, passing five or six times from one to the other before I was exhausted. In the intervals, seeing them to be docile and desirous, I made them execute Aretin's most complicated postures, which amused them beyond words. We kissed whatever took our fancy, and just as Hedvig applied her lips to the mouth of the pistol, it went off and the discharge inundated her face and her bosom. She was delighted, and watched the process to the end with all the curiosity of a doctor. The night seemed short, though we had not lost a moment's time, and at daybreak we had to part. I left them in bed and I was fortunate enough to get away without being observed.

I slept till noon, and then having made my toilette I went to call on the pastor, to whom I praised Hedvig to the skies. This was the best way to get him to come to supper at Balances the next day.

"We shall be in the town," said I, "and can remain together as long as we please, but do not forget to bring the amiable widow and her charming daughter."

He promised he would bring them both.

In the evening I went to see the syndic and his three friends, who naturally found me rather insensible to their charms. I excused myself by saying that I had a bad headache. I told them that I had asked the young theologian to supper, and invited the girls and the syndic to come too; but, as I had foreseen, the latter would not hear of their going as it would give rise to gossip.

I took care that the most exquisite wines should form an important feature of my supper. The pastor and the widow were both sturdy drinkers, and I did my best to please them. When I saw that they were pretty mellow and were going over their old recollections, I made a sign to the girls, and they immediately went out as if to go to a retiring-room. Under pretext of shewing them the way I went out too, and took them into a room telling them to wait for me.

I went back to the supper-room, and finding the old friends taken up with each other and scarcely conscious of my presence, I gave them some punch, and told them that I would keep the young ladies company; they were looking at some pictures, I explained. I lost no time, and shewed them some extremely interesting sights. These stolen sweets have a wonderful charm. When we were to some extent satisfied, we went back, and I plied the punch-ladle more and more freely. Helen praised the pictures to her mother, and asked her to come and look at them.

"I don't care to," she replied.

"Well," said Helen, "let us go and see them again."

I thought this stratagem admissible, and going out with my two sweethearts I worked wonders. Hedvig philosophised over pleasure, and told me she would never have known it if I had not chanced to meet her uncle. Helen did not speak; she was more voluptuous than her cousin, and swelled out like a dove, and came to life only to expire a moment afterwards. I wondered at her astonishing fecundity; while I was engaged in one operation she passed from death to life fourteen times. It is true that it was the sixth time with me, so I made my progress rather slower to enjoy the pleasure she took in it.

Before we parted I agreed to call on Helen's mother every day to ascertain the night I could spend with them before I left Geneva. We broke up our party at two o'clock in the morning.

Three or four days after, Helen told me briefly that Hedvig was to sleep with her that night, and that she would leave the door open at the same time as before.

"I will be there."

"And I will be there to shut you up, but you cannot have a light as the servant might see it."

I was exact to the time, and when ten o'clock struck they came to fetch me in high glee.

"I forgot to tell you," said Helen, "that you would find a fowl there."

I felt hungry, and made short work of it, and then we gave ourselves up to happiness.

I had to set out on my travels in two days. I had received a couple of letters from M. Raiberti. In the first he told me that he had followed my instructions as to the Corticelli, and in the second that she would probably he paid for dancing at the carnival as first 'figurante'. I had nothing to keep me at Geneva, and Madame d'Urfe, according to our agreement, would be waiting for me at Lyons. I was therefore obliged to go there. Thus the night that I was to pass with my two charmers would be my last.

My lessons had taken effect, and I found they had become past mistresses in the art of pleasure. But now and again joy gave place to sadness.

"We shall be wretched, sweetheart," said Hedvig, "and if you like we will come with you."

"I promise to come and see you before two years have expired," said I; and in fact they had not so long to wait.

We fell asleep at midnight, and waking at four renewed our sweet battles till six o'clock. Half an hour after I left them, worn out with my exertions, and I remained in bed all day. In the evening I went to see the syndic and his young friends. I found Helen there, and she was cunning enough to feign not to be more vexed at my departure than the others, and to further the deception she allowed the syndic to kiss her. I followed suit, and begged her to bid farewell for me to her learned cousin and to excuse my taking leave of her in person.

The next day I set out in the early morning, and on the following day I reached Lyons. Madame d'Urfe was not there, she had gone to an estate of hers at Bresse. I found a letter in which she said that she would be delighted to see me, and I waited on her without losing any time.

She greeted me with her ordinary cordiality, and I told her that I was going to Turin to meet Frederic Gualdo, the head of the

Fraternity of the Rosy Cross, and I revealed to her by the oracle that he would come with me to Marseilles, and that there he would complete her happiness. After having received this oracle she would not go to Paris before she saw us. The oracle also bade her wait for me at Lyons with young d'Aranda; who begged me to take him with me to Turin. It may be imagined that I succeeded in putting him off.

Madame d'Urfe had to wait a fortnight to get me fifty thousand francs which I might require on my journey. In the course of this fortnight I made the acquaintance of Madame Pernon, and spent a good deal of money with her husband, a rich mercer, in refurnishing my wardrobe. Madame Pernon was handsome and intelligent. She had a Milanese lover, named Bono, who did business for a Swiss banker named Sacco. It was through Madame Peron that Bono got Madame d'Urfe the fifty thousand francs I required. She also gave me the three dresses which she had promised to the Countess of Lascaris, but which that lady had never seen.

One of these dresses was furred, and was exquisitely beautiful. I left Lyons equipped like a prince, and journeyed towards Turin, where I was to meet the famous Gualdo, who was none other than Ascanio Pogomas, whom I had summoned from Berne. I thought it would be easy to make the fellow play the part I had destined for him, but I was cruelly deceived as the reader will see.

I could not resist stopping at Chamberi to see my fair nun, whom I found looking beautiful and contented. She was grieving, however, after the young boarder, who had been taken from the convent and married.

I got to Turin at the beginning of December, and at Rivoli I found the Corticelli, who had been warned by the Chevalier de Raiberti of my arrival. She gave me a letter from this worthy gentleman, giving the address of the house he had taken for me as I did not want to put up at an inn. I immediately went to take possession of my new lodging.

CHAPTER XVII

My Old Friends—Pacienza—Agatha—Count Boryomeo—The Ball—Lord Percy

The Corticelli was as gentle as a lamb, and left me as we got into Turin. I promised I would come and see her, and immediately went to the house the Chevalier had taken, which I found convenient in every way.

The worthy Chevalier was not long in calling on me. He gave me an account of the moneys he had spent on the Corticelli, and handed over the rest to me.

"I am flush of money," I said, "and I intend to invite my friends to supper frequently. Can you lay your hands on a good cook?"

"I know a pearl amongst cooks," said he, "and you can have him directly."

"You, chevalier, are the pearl of men. Get me this wonder, tell him I am hard to please, and agree on the sum I am to pay him per month."

The cook, who was an excellent one, came the same evening.

"It would be a good idea," said Raiberti, "to call on the Count d'Aglie. He knows that the Corticelli is your mistress, and he has given a formal order to Madame Pacienza, the lady with whom she lives, that when you come and see her you are not to be left alone together."

This order amused me, and as I did not care about the Corticelli it did not trouble me in the least, though Raiberti, who thought I was in love with her, seemed to pity me.

"Since she has been here," he said, "her conduct has been irreproachable."

"I am glad to hear that."

"You might let her take some lessons from the dancing-master Dupre," said he. "He will no doubt give her something to do at the carnival."

I promised to follow his advice, and I then paid a visit to the superintendent of police.

He received me well, complimented me on my return to Turin, and then added with a smile:—

"I warn you that I have been informed that you keep a mistress, and that I have given strict orders to the respectable woman with whom she lives not to leave her alone with you."

"I am glad to hear it," I replied, "and the more as I fear her mother is not a person of very rigid morals. I advised the Chevalier Raiberti of my intentions with regard to her, and I am glad to see that he has carried them out so well. I hope the girl will shew herself worthy of your protection."

"Do you think of staying here throughout the carnival?"

"Yes, if your excellency approves."

"It depends entirely on your good conduct."

"A few peccadilloes excepted, my conduct is always above reproach."

"There are some peccadilloes we do not tolerate here. Have you seen the

Chevalier Osorio?"

"I think of calling on him to-day or to-morrow."

"I hope you will remember me to him."

He rang his bell, bowed, and the audience was over.

The Chevalier Osorio received me at his office, and gave me a most gracious reception. After I had given him an account of my visit to the superintendent, he asked me, with a smile, if I felt inclined to submit with docility to not seeing my mistress in freedom.

"Certainly," said I, "for I am not in love with her."

Osorio looked at me slyly, and observed, "Somehow I don't think your indifference will be very pleasing to the virtuous duenna."

I understood what he meant, but personally I was delighted not to be able to see the Corticelli save in the presence of a female dragon. It would make people talk, and I loved a little scandal, and felt curious to see what would happen.

When I returned to my house I found the Genoese Passano, a bad poet and worse painter, to whom I had intended to give the part of a Rosicrucian, because there was something in his appearance which inspired, if not respect, at least awe and a certain feeling of fear. In point of fact, this was only a natural presentiment that the man must be either a clever rogue or a morose and sullen scholar.

I made him sup with me and gave him a room on the third floor, telling him not to leave it without my permission. At supper I found him insipid in conversation, drunken, ignorant, and ill disposed, and I already repented of having taken him under my protection; but the thing was done.

The next day, feeling curious to see how the Corticelli was lodged, I called on her, taking with me a piece of Lyons silk.

I found her and her mother in the landlady's room, and as I came in the latter said that she was delighted to see me and that she hoped I would often dine with them. I thanked her briefly and spoke to the girl coolly enough.

"Shew me your room," said I. She took me there in her mother's company. "Here is something to make you a winter dress," said I, shewing her the silk.

"Is this from the marchioness?"

"No, it is from me."

"But where are the three dresses she said she would give me?"

"You know very well on what conditions you were to have them, so let us say no more about it."

She unfolded the silk which she liked very much, but she said she must have some trimmings. The Pacienza offered her services, and said she would send for a dressmaker who lived close by. I acquiesced with a nod, and as soon as she had left the room the Signora Laura said she was very sorry only to be able to receive me in the presence of the landlady.

"I should have thought," said I, "that a virtuous person like you would have been delighted."

"I thank God for it every morning and night."

"You infernal old hypocrite!" said I, looking contemptuously at her.

"Upon my word, anybody who didn't know you would be taken in."

In a few minutes Victorine and another girl came in with their band-boxes.

"Are you still at Madame R——'s?" said I.

"Yes sir," said she, with a blush.

When the Corticelli had chosen what she wanted I told Victorine to present my compliments to her mistress, and tell her that I would call and pay for the articles.

The landlady had also sent for a dressmaker, and while the Corticelli was being measured, she shewed me her figure and said she wanted a corset. I jested on the pregnancy with which she threatened me, and of which there was now no trace, pitying Count N—— for being deprived of the joys of fatherhood. I then gave her what money she required and took my leave. She escorted me to the door, and asked me if she should have the pleasure of seeing me again before long.

"It's a pleasure, is it?" I replied; "well, I don't know when you will have it again; it depends on my leisure and my fancy."

It is certain that if I had any amorous feelings or even curiosity about the girl, I should not have left her in that house for a moment; but I repeat my love for her had entirely vanished. There was one thing, however, which annoyed me intolerably, namely, that in spite of my coolness towards her, the little hussy pretended to think that I had forgotten and forgiven everything.

On leaving the Corticelli, I proceeded to call on my bankers, amongst others on M. Martin, whose wife was justly famous for her wit and beauty.

I chanced to meet the horse-dealing Jew, who had made money out of me by means of his daughter Leah. She was still pretty, but married; and her figure was too rounded for my taste. She and her husband welcomed me with great warmth, but I cared for her no longer, and did not wish to see her again.

I called on Madame R——, who had been awaiting me impatiently ever since Victorine had brought news of me. I sat down by the counter and had the pleasure of hearing from her lips the amorous histories of Turin for the past few months.

"Victorine and Caton are the only two of the old set that still remain, but I have replaced them with others."

"Has Victorine found anyone to operate on her yet?"

"No, she is just as you left her, but a gentleman who is in love with her is going to take her to Milan."

This gentleman was the Comte de Perouse, whose acquaintance I made three years afterwards at Milan. I shall speak of him in due time. Madame R—— told me that, in consequence of her getting into trouble several times with the police, she had been obliged to promise the Count d'Aglie only to send the girls to ladies, and, consequently, if I found any of them to my taste I should be obliged to make friends with their relations and take them to the festas. She shewed me the girls in the work-room, but I did not think any of them worth taking trouble about.

She talked about the Pacienza, and when I told her that I kept the Corticelli, and of the hard conditions to which I was obliged to submit, she exclaimed with astonishment, and amused me by her jests on the subject.

"You are in good hands, my dear sir," said she; "the woman is not only a spy of d'Aglie's, but a professional procuress. I wonder the Chevalier Raiberti placed the girl with her."

She was not so surprised when I told her that the chevalier had good reasons for his action, and that I myself had good reasons of my own for wishing the Corticelli to remain there.

Our conversation was interrupted by a customer who wanted silk stockings. Hearing him speak of dancing, I asked him if he could tell me the address of Dupre, the ballet-master.

"No one better, sir, for I am Dupre, at your service."

"I am delighted at this happy chance. The Chevalier Raiberti gave me to understand that you might be able to give dancing lessons to a ballet-girl of my acquaintance."

"M. de Raiberti mentioned your name to me this morning. You must be the Chevalier de Seingalt?"

"Exactly."

"I can give the young lady lessons every morning at nine o'clock at my own home."

"No, do you come to her house, but at whatever hour you like. I will pay you, and I hope you will make her one of your best pupils. I must warn you, however, that she is not a novice."

"I will call on her to-day, and to-morrow I will tell you what I can make of her; but I think I had better tell you my terms: I charge three Piedmontese livres a lesson."

"I think that is very reasonable; I will call on you to-morrow."

"You do me honour. Here is my address. If you like to come in the afternoon you will see the rehearsal of a ballet."

"Is it not rehearsed at the theatre?"

"Yes, but at the theatre no on-lookers are allowed by the orders of the superintendent of police."

"This superintendent of yours puts his finger into a good many pies."

"In too many."

"But at your own house anybody may come?"

"Undoubtedly, but I could not have the dancers there if my wife were not present. The superintendent knows her, and has great confidence in her."

"You will see me at the rehearsal."

The wretched superintendent had erected a fearful system of surveillance against the lovers of pleasure, but it must be confessed that he was often cheated. Voluptuousness was all the more rampant when thus restrained; and so it ever will be while men have passions and women desires. To love and enjoy, to desire and to satisfy one's desires, such is the circle in which we move, and whence we can never be turned. When restrictions are placed upon the passions as in Turkey, they still attain their ends, but by methods destructive to morality.

At the worthy Mazzali's I found two gentlemen to whom she introduced me. One was old and ugly, decorated with the Order of the White Eagle—his name was Count Borromeo; the other, young and brisk, was Count A—— B—— of Milan. After they had gone I was informed that they were paying assiduous court to the

Chevalier Raiberti, from whom they hoped to obtain certain privileges for their lordships which were under the Sardinian rule.

The Milanese count had not a penny, and the Lord of the Borromean Isles was not much better off. He had ruined himself with women, and not being able to live at Milan he had taken refuge in the fairest of his isles, and enjoyed there perpetual spring and very little else. I paid him a visit on my return from Spain, but I shall relate our meeting when I come to my adventures, my pleasures, my misfortunes, and above all my follies there, for of such threads was the weft of my life composed, and folly was the prominent element.

The conversation turned on my house, and the lively Mazzoli asked me how I liked my cook. I replied that I had not yet tried him, but I proposed to put him to test the next day, if she and the gentlemen would do me the honour of supping with me.

The invitation was accepted, and she promised to bring her dear chevalier with her, and to warn him of the event, as his health only allowed him to eat once a day.

I called on Dupre in the afternoon. I saw the dancers, male and female, the latter accompanied by their mothers, who stood on one side muffled up in thick cloaks. As I passed them under review in my lordly manner, I noticed that one of them still looked fresh and pretty, which augured well for her daughter, though the fruit does not always correspond to the tree.

Dupre introduced me to his wife, who was young and pretty, but who had been obliged to leave the theatre owing to the weakness of her chest. She told me that if the Corticelli would work hard her husband would make a great dancer of her, as her figure was eminently suited for dancing. While I was talking with Madame Dupre, the Corticelli, late Lascaris, came running up to me with the air of a favourite, and told me she wanted some ribbons and laces to make a bonnet. The others girls began to whisper to each other, and guessing what they must be saying I turned to Dupre without taking any notice of Madame Madcap, and gave him twelve pistoles, saying that I would pay for the lessons three months in advance, and that I hoped he would bring his new pupil on well. Such a heavy payment in advance caused general surprise, which I enjoyed, though pretending not to be aware of it. Now I know that I acted foolishly, but I have promised to speak the truth in these Memoirs, which will not see the light till all light has left my eyes, and I will keep my promise.

I have always been greedy of distinction; I have always loved to draw the eyes of men towards men, but I must also add that if I have humiliated anyone it has always been a proud man or a fool, for it has been my rule to please everyone if I can.

I sat on one side, the better to observe the swarm of girls, and I soon fixed my eyes on one whose appearance struck me. She had a fine figure, delicate features, a noble air, and a patient look which interested me in the highest degree. She was dancing with a man who did not scruple to abuse her in the coarsest manner when she made any mistakes, but she bore it without replying, though an expression of contempt mingled with the sweetness of her face.

Instinct drew me to the mother I have remarked on, and I asked her to whom the dancer that interested me belonged.

"I am her mother," she replied.

"You, madam! I should not have thought it possible."

"I was very young when she was born."

"I should think so. Where do you come from?"

"I am from Lucca, and what is more-a poor widow."

"How can you be poor, when you are still young and handsome, and have an angel for a daughter?"

She replied only by an expressive glance. I understood her reserve, and I stayed by her without speaking. Soon after, Agatha, as her daughter was named, came up to her to ask for a handkerchief to wipe her face.

"Allow me to offer you mine," said I. Il was a white handkerchief, and scented with attar of roses; this latter circumstance gave her an excuse for accepting it, but after smelling it she wanted to return it to me.

"You have not used it," said I! "do so."

She obeyed, and then returned it to me with a bow by way of thanks.

"You must not give it me back, fair Agatha, till you have had it washed."

She smiled, and gave it to her mother, glancing at me in a grateful manner, which I considered of good omen.

"May I have the pleasure of calling on you?" said I. "I cannot receive you, sir, except in the presence of my landlady."

"This cursed restriction is general in Turin, then?"

"Yes, the superintendent uses everybody in the same way."

"Then I shall have the pleasure of seeing you again here?"

In the evening I had one of the best suppers I ever had in my life, if I except those I enjoyed during my stay at Turin. My cook was worthy of a place in the kitchen of Lucullus; but without detracting from his skill I must do justice to the products of the country. Everything is delicious; game, fish, birds, meat, vegetables, fruit, milk, and truffles—all are worthy of the table of the greatest gourmets, and the wines of the country yield to none. What a pity that strangers do not enjoy liberty at Turin! It is true that better society, and more politeness, such as are found in several French and Italian towns, are to be wished for.

The beauty of the women of Turin is no doubt due to the excellence of the air and diet.

I had not much trouble in extracting a promise from Madame Mazzoli and the two counts to sup with me every night, but the Chevalier de Raiberti would only promise to come whenever he could.

At the Carignan Theatre, where opera-bouffe was being played, I saw Redegonde, with whom I had failed at Florence. She saw me in the pit and gave me a smile, so I wrote to her, offering my services if the mother had changed her way of thinking. She answered that her mother was always the same, but that if I would ask the Corticelli she could come and sup with me, though the mother would doubtless have to be of the party. I gave her no answer, as the terms she named were by no means to my taste.

I had a letter from Madame du Rumain, enclosing one from M. de Choiseul to M. de Chauvelin, the French ambassador at Turin. It will be remembered that I had known this worthy nobleman at Soleure, and had been treated with great politeness by him, but I wished to have a more perfect title to his acquaintance; hence I asked Madame du Rumain to give me a letter.

M. de Chauvelin received me with the greatest cordiality; and reproaching me for having thought a letter of introduction necessary, introduced me to his charming wife, who was no less kind than her husband. Three or four days later he asked me to dine with him, and I met at his table M. Imberti, the Venetian ambassador, who said he was very sorry not to be able to present me at Court. On hearing the reason M. de Chauvelin offered to present me himself, but I thought it best to decline with thanks. No doubt it would have been a great honour, but the result would be that I should be more spied on than even in this town of spies, where the most indifferent actions do not pass unnoticed. My pleasures would have been interfered with.

Count Borromeo continued to honour me by coming every night to sup with me, preserving his dignity the while, for as he accompanied Madame Mazzoli it was not to be supposed that he came because he was in need of a meal. Count A—— B—— came more frankly, and I was pleased with him. He told me one day that the way I put up with his visits made him extremely grateful to Providence, for his wife could not send him any money, and he could not afford to pay for his dinner at the inn, so that if it were not for my kindness he would often be obliged to go hungry to bed. He shewed me his wife's letters; he had evidently a high opinion of her. "I hope," he would say, "that you will come and stay with us at Milan, and that she will please you."

He had been in the service of Spain, and by what he said I judged his wife to be a pleasing brunette of twenty-five or twenty-six. The count had told her how I had lent him money several times, and of my goodness to him, and she replied, begging him to express her gratitude to me, and to make me promise to stay with them at Milan. She wrote wittily, and her letters interested me to such an extent that I gave a formal promise to journey to Milan, if it were only for the sake of seeing her.

I confess that in doing so I was overcome by my feelings of curiosity. I knew they were poor, and I should not have given a promise which would either bring them into difficulties or expose me to paying too dearly for my lodging. However, by way of excuse, I can only say that curiosity is near akin to love. I fancied the countess sensible like an Englishwoman, passionate like a Spaniard, caressing like a Frenchwoman, and as I had a good enough opinion of my own merit, I did not doubt for a moment that she would respond to my affection. With these pleasant delusions in my head, I counted on exciting the jealousy of all the ladies and gentlemen of Milan. I had plenty of money, and I longed for an opportunity of spending it.

Nevertheless, I went every day to rehearsal at Dupre's, and I soon got madly in love with Agatha. Madame Dupre won over by several presents I made her, received my confidences with kindness, and by asking Agatha and her mother to dinner procured me the pleasure of a more private meeting with my charmer. I profited by the opportunity to make known my feelings, and I obtained some slight favours, but so slight were they that my flame only grew the fiercer.

Agatha kept on telling me that everybody knew that the Corticelli was my mistress, and that for all the gold in the world she would not have it said that she was my last shift, as I could not see the Corticelli in private. I swore to her that I did not love the Corticelli, and that I only kept her to prevent M. Raiberti being compromised; but all this was of no avail, she had formed her plans, and nothing would content her but a formal rupture which would give all Turin to understand that I loved her and her alone. On these conditions she promised me her heart, and everything which follows in such cases.

I loved her too well not to endeavour to satisfy her, since my satisfaction depended on hers. With this idea I got Dupre to give a ball at my expense in some house outside the town, and to invite all the dancers, male and female, who were engaged for the carnival at Turin. Every gentleman had the right to bring a lady to have supper and look on, as only the professional dancers were allowed to dance.

I told Dupre that I would look after the refreshment department, and that he might tell everybody that no expense was to be spared. I also provided carriages and sedan-chairs for the ladies, but nobody was to know that I was furnishing the money. Dupre saw that there was profit in store for him, and went about it at once. He found a suitable house, asked the lady dancers, and distributed about fifty tickets.

Agatha and her mother were the only persons who knew that the project was mine, and that I was responsible to a great extent for the expenses; but these facts were generally known the day after the ball.

Agatha had no dress that was good enough, so I charged Madame Dupre to provide one at my expense, and I was well served. It is well known that when this sort of people dip their fingers into other's purses they are not sparing, but that was just what I wanted. Agatha promised to dance all the quadrilles with me, and to return to Turin with Madame Dupre.

On the day fixed for the ball I stayed to dinner at the Dupre's to be present at Agatha's toilette. Her dress was a rich and newly-made Lyons silk, and the trimming was exquisite Alencon point lace, of which the girl did not know the value. Madame R——, who had arranged the dress, and Madame Dupre, had received instructions to say nothing about it to her.

When Agatha was ready to start, I told her that the ear-rings she was wearing were not good enough for her dress.

"That's true," said Madame Dupre, "and it's a great pity."

"Unfortunately," said the mother, "my poor girl hasn't got another pair."

"I have some pretty imitation pendants, which I could lend you," said I; "they are really very brilliant."

I had taken care to put the ear-rings which Madame d'Urfe had intended for the Countess Lascaris in my pocket. I drew them out, and they were greatly admired.

"One would swear they were real diamonds," said Madame Dupre.

I put them in Agatha's ears. She admired them very much, and said that all the other girls would be jealous, as they would certainly take them for real stones.

I went home and made an elaborate toilette, and on arriving at the ball I found Agatha dancing with Lord Percy, a young fool, who was the son of the Duke of Northumberland, and an extravagant spendthrift.

I noticed several handsome ladies from Turin, who, being merely onlookers, might be thinking that the ball was given for their amusement, like the fly on the chariot wheel. All the ambassadors were present, and amongst others M. de Chauvelin, who told me that to make everything complete my pretty housekeeper at Soleure was wanting.

The Marquis and Marchioness de Prie were there also. The marquis did not care to dance, so was playing a little game of quinze with a rude gamester, who would not let the marquis's mistress look over his cards. She saw me, but pretended not to recognize me; the trick I had played her at Aix being probably enough to last her for some time.

The minuets came to an end, and Dupre announced the quadrilles, and I was glad to see the Chevalier Ville-Follet dancing with the Corticelli. My partner was Agatha, who had great difficulty in getting rid of Lord Percy, though she told him that she was fully engaged.

Minuets and quadrilles followed each other in succession, and refreshments began to make their appearance. I was delighted to see that the refreshment counter was furnished with the utmost liberality. The Piedmontese, who are great at calculations, estimated that Dupre must lose by it, the firing of champagne corks was continuous.

Feeling tired I asked Agatha to sit down, and I was telling her how I loved her when Madame de Chauvelin and another lady interrupted us. I rose to give them place, and Agatha imitated my example; but Madame de Chauvelin made her sit down beside her, and praised her dress, and above all the lace trimming. The other lady said how pretty her ear-rings were, and what a pity it was that those imitation stones would lose their brilliance in time. Madame de Chauvelin, who knew something about precious stones, said that they would never lose their brilliance, as they were diamonds of the first water.

"It is not so?" she added, to Agatha, who in the candour of her heart confessed that they were imitation, and that I had lent them to her.

At this Madame de Chauvelin burst out laughing, and said,—

"M. de Seingalt has deceived you, my dear child. A gentleman of his caste does not lend imitation jewellery to such a pretty girl as you are. Your ear-rings are set with magnificent diamonds."

She blushed, for my silence confirmed the lady's assertion, and she felt that the fact of my having lent her such stones was a palpable proof of the great esteem in which I held her.

Madame de Chauvelin asked me to dance a minuet with Agatha, and my partner executed the dance with wonderful grace. When it was over Madame de Chauvelin thanked me, and told me that she should always remember our dancing together at Soleure, and that she hoped I would dance again with her at her own house. A profound bow shewed her how flattered I felt by the compliment.

The ball did not come to an end till four o'clock in the morning, and I did not leave it till I saw Agatha going away in the company with Madame Dupre.

I was still in bed the next morning, when my man told me a pretty woman wanted to speak to me. I had her in and was delighted to find it was Agatha's mother. I made her sit down beside me, and gave her a cup of chocolate. As soon as we were alone she drew my ear-rings from her pocket, and said, with a smile, that she had just been shewing them to a jeweller, who had offered her a thousand sequins for them.

"The man's mad," said I, "you ought to have let him have them; they are not worth four sequins."

So saying, I drew her to my arms and gave her a kiss. Feeling that she had shared in the kiss, and that she seemed to like it, I went farther, and at last we spent a couple of hours in shewing what a high opinion we had of each other.

Afterwards we both looked rather astonished, and it was the beautiful mother who first broke the silence.

"Am I to tell my girl," said she, with a smile, "of the way in which you proved to me that you love her?"

"I leave that to your discretion, my dear," said I. "I have certainly proved that I love you, but it does not follow that I do not adore your daughter. In fact, I burn for her; and yet, if we are not careful to avoid being alone together, what has just happened between us will often happen again."

"It is hard to resist you, and it is possible that I may have occasion to speak to you again in private."

"You may be sure you will always be welcome, and all I ask of you is not to put any obstacles in the way of my suit with Agatha."

"I have also a favour to ask."

"If it is within my power, you may be sure I will grant it."

"Very good! Then tell me if these ear-rings are real, and what was your intention in putting them in my daughter's ears?"

"The diamonds are perfectly genuine, and my intention was that Agatha should keep them as a proof of my affection."

She heaved a sigh, and then told me that I might ask them to supper, with Dupre and his wife, whenever I pleased. I thanked her, gave her ten sequins, and sent her away happy.

On reflection I decided that I had never seen a more sensible woman than Agatha's mother. It would have been impossible to announce the success of my suit in a more delicate or more perspicuous manner.

My readers will no doubt guess that I seized the opportunity and brought this interesting affair to a conclusion. The same evening I asked Dupre and his wife, Agatha and her mother, to sup with me the next day, in addition to my usual company. But as I was leaving Dupre's I had an adventure.

My man, who was a great rascal, but who behaved well on this occasion, ran up to me panting for breath, and said triumphantly,

"Sir, I have been looking for you to warn you that I have just seen the Chevalier de Ville-Follet slip into Madame Pacienza's house, and I suspect he is making an amorous call on the Corticelli."

I immediately walked to the abode of the worthy spy in high spirits, and hoping that my servant's guess had been correct. I walked in and found the landlady and the mother sitting together. Without noticing them, I was making my way towards the Corticelli's room when the two old ladies arrested my course, telling me that the signora was not well and wanted rest. I pushed them aside, and entered the room so swiftly and suddenly that I found the gentleman in a state of nature while the girl remained stretched on the bed as if petrified by my sudden apparition.

"Sir," said I, "I hope you will pardon me for coming in without knocking."

"Wait a moment, wait a moment."

Far from waiting I went away in high glee, and told the story to the Chevalier Raiberti, who enjoyed it as well as I did. I asked him to warn the Pacienza woman that from that day I would pay nothing for Corticelli, who had ceased to belong to me. He approved, and said,—

"I suppose you will not be going to complain to the Count d'Aglie?"

"It is only fools who complain, above all in circumstances like these."

This scandalous story would have been consigned to forgetfulness, if it had not been for the Chevalier de Ville-Follet's indiscretion. He felt angry at being interrupted in the middle of the business, and remembering he had seen my man just before fixed on him as the informer. Meeting him in the street the chevalier reproached him for spying, whereon the impudent rascal replied that he was only answerable to his master, and that it was his duty to serve me in all things. On this the chevalier caned him, and the man went to complain to the superintendent, who summoned Ville-Follet to appear before him and explain his conduct. Having nothing to fear, he told the whole story.

The Chevalier de Raiberti, too, was very ill received when he went to tell Madame Pacienza that neither he nor I were going to pay her anything more in future; but he would listen to no defence. The chevalier came to sup with me, and he informed me that on leaving the house he had met a police sergeant, whom he concluded had come to cite the landlady to appear before the Count d'Aglie.

The next day, just as I was going to M. de Chauvelin's ball, I received to my great surprise a note from the superintendent begging me to call on him as he had something to communicate to me. I immediately ordered my chairmen to take me to his residence.

M. de Aglie received me in private with great politeness, and after giving me a chair he began a long and pathetic discourse, the gist of which was that it was my duty to forgive this little slip of my mistress's.

"That's exactly what I am going to do," said I; "and for the rest of my days I never wish to see the Corticelli again, or to make or mar in her affairs, and for all this I am greatly obliged to the Chevalier de Ville-Follet."

159

"I see you are angry. Come, come! you must not abandon the girl for that. I will have the woman Pacienza punished in such a way as to satisfy you, and I will place the girl in a respectable family where you can go and see her in perfect liberty."

"I am greatly obliged to you for your kindness, indeed I am grateful; but I despise the Pacienza too heartily to wish for her punishment, and as to the Corticelli and her mother, they are two female swindlers, who have given me too much trouble already. I am well quit of them."

"You must confess, however, that you had no right to make a forcible entry into a room in a house which does not belong to you."

"I had not the right, I confess, but if I had not taken it I could never have had a certain proof of the perfidy of my mistress; and I should have been obliged to continue supporting her, though she entertained other lovers."

"The Corticelli pretends that you are her debtor, and not vice versa. She says that the diamonds you have given another girl belong of right to her, and that Madame d'Urfe, whom I have the honour to know, presented her with them."

"She is a liar! And as you know Madame d'Urfe, kindly write to her (she is at Lyons); and if the marchioness replies that I owe the wretched girl anything, be sure that I will discharge the debt. I have a hundred thousand francs in good banks of this town, and the money will be a sufficient surety for the ear-rings I have disposed of."

"I am sorry that things have happened so."

"And I am very glad, as I have ridden myself of a burden that was hard to bear."

Thereupon we bowed politely to one another, and I left the office.

At the French ambassador's ball I heard so much talk of my adventure that at last I refused to reply to any more questions on the subject. The general opinion was that the whole affair was a trifle of which I could not honourably take any notice; but I thought myself the best judge of my own honour, and was determined to take no notice of the opinions of others. The Chevalier de Ville-Follet came up to me and said that if I abandoned the Corticelli for such a trifle, he should feel obliged to give me satisfaction. I shook his hand, saying,—

"My dear chevalier, it will be enough if you do not demand satisfaction of me."

I te understood how the land lay, and said no more about it; but not so his sister, the Marchioness de Prie, who made a vigorous attack on me after we had danced together. She was handsome, and might have been victorious if she had liked, but luckily she did not think of exerting her power, and so gained nothing.

Three days after, Madame de St. Giles, a great power in Turin, and a kind of protecting deity to all actresses, summoned me to her presence by a liveried footman. Guessing what she wanted, I called on her unceremoniously in a morning coat. She received me politely, and began to talk of the Corticelli affair with great affability; but I did not like her, and replied dryly that I had had no hesitation in abandoning the girl to the protection of the gallant gentleman with whom I had surprised her in 'flagrante delicto'. She told me I should be sorry for it, and that she would publish a little story which she had already read and which did not do me much credit. I replied that I never changed my mind, and that threats were of no avail with me. With that parting shot I left her.

I did not attach much importance to the town gossip, but a week after I received a manuscript containing an account—accurate in most respects—of my relations with the Corticelli and Madame d'Urfe, but so ill written and badly expressed that nobody could read it without weariness. It did not make the slightest impression on me, and I stayed a fortnight longer in Turin without its causing me the slightest annoyance. I saw the Corticelli again in Paris six months after, and will speak of our meeting in due time.

The day after M. de Chauvelin's ball I asked Agatha, her mother, the Dupres, and my usual company to supper. It was the mother's business to so arrange matters that the ear-rings should become Agatha's lawful property, so I left everything to her. I knew she would manage to introduce the subject, and while we were at supper she said that the common report of Turin was that I had given her daughter a pair of diamond ear-rings worth five hundred Louis, which the Corticelli claimed as hers by right.

"I do not know," she added, "if they are real diamonds, or if they belong to the Corticelli, but I do know that my girl has received no such present from the gentleman."

"Well, well," said I, "we will have no more surmises in the matter;" and going up to Agatha I put the earrings on her, saying,—

"Dearest Agatha, I make you a present of them before this company, and my giving them to you now is a proof that hitherto they have belonged to me."

Everybody applauded, and I read in the girl's eyes that I should have no cause to regret my generosity.

We then fell to speaking of the affair of Ville-Follet and the Corticelli, and of the efforts that had been made to compel me to retain her. The Chevalier Raiberti said that in my place he would have offered Madame de St. Giles or the superintendent to continue paying for her board, but merely as an act of charity, and that I could have deposited money with either of them.

"I should be very glad to do so," said I; and the next day the worthy chevalier made the necessary arrangements with Madame de St. Giles, and I furnished the necessary moneys.

In spite of this charitable action, the wretched manuscript came out, but, as I have said, without doing me any harm. The superintendent made the Corticelli live in the same house with Redegonde, and Madame Pacienza was left in peace.

After supper, with the exception of the Chevalier Raiberti, we all masked, and went to the ball at the opera-house. I soon seized the opportunity of escaping with Agatha, and she granted me all that love can desire. All constraint was banished; she was my titular mistress, and we were proud of belonging the one to the other, for we loved each other. The suppers I had given at my house had set me perfectly at liberty, and the superintendent could do nothing to thwart our love, though he was informed of it, so well are the spies of Turin organized.

Divine Providence made use of me as its instrument in making Agatha's fortune. It may be said that Providence might have chosen a more moral method, but are we to presume to limit the paths of Providence to the narrow circle of our prejudices and conventions? It has its own ways, which often appear dark to us because of our ignorance. At all events, if I am able to continue these Memoirs for six or seven years more, the reader will see that Agatha shewed herself grateful. But to return to our subject.

The happiness we enjoyed by day and night was so great, Agatha was so affectionate and I so amorous, that we should certainly have remained united for some time if it had not been for the event I am about to relate. It made me leave Turin much sooner than I had intended, for I had not purposed to visit the wonderful Spanish countess at Milan till Lent. The husband of the Spanish lady had finished his business and left Turin, thanking me with tears in his eyes; and if it had not been for me he would not have been able to quit the town, for I paid divers small debts he had incurred, and gave him the wherewithal for his journey. Often is vice thus found allied to virtue or masking in virtue's guise; but what matter? I allowed myself to be taken in, and did not wish to be disabused. I do not seek to conceal my faults. I have always led a profligate life, and have not always been very delicate in the choice of means to gratify my passions, but even amidst my vices I was always a passionate lover of virtue. Benevolence, especially, has always had a great charm for me, and I have never failed to exercise it unless when restrained by the desire of vengeance—a vice which has always had a controlling influence on my actions.

Lord Percy, as I have remarked, was deeply in love with my Agatha. He followed her about everywhere, was present at all the rehearsals, waited for her at the wings, and called on her every day, although her landlady, a duenna of the Pacienza school, would never let her see him alone. The principal methods of seduction—rich presents—had not been spared, but Agatha persistently refused them all, and forbade her duenna to take anything from the young nobleman. Agatha had no liking for him, and kept me well informed of all his actions, and we used to laugh at him together. I knew that I possessed her heart, and consequently Lord Percy's attempts neither made me angry or jealous—nay, they flattered my self-esteem, for his slighted love made my own happiness stand out in greater relief. Everybody knew that Agatha remained faithful to me, and at last Lord Percy was so convinced of the hopelessness of the attempt that he resolved on making a friend of me, and winning me over to his interests.

With the true Englishman's boldness and coolness he came to me one morning, and asked me to give him breakfast. I welcomed him in the French manner, that is, with combined cordiality and politeness, and he was soon completely at his ease.

With insular directness he went straight to the point at the first interview, declared his love for Agatha, and proposed an exchange, which amused, but did not offend me, as I knew that such bargains were common in England.

"I know," said he, "that you are in love with Redegonde, and have long tried vainly to obtain her; now I am willing to exchange her for Agatha, and all I want to know is what sum of money you want over and above?"

"You are very good, my dear lord, but to determine the excess of value would require a good mathematician. Redegonde is all very well, and inspires me with curiosity, but what is she compared to Agatha?"

"I know, I know, and I therefore offer you any sum you like to mention."

Percy was very rich, and very passionate. I am sure that if I had named twenty-five thousand guineas as overplus, or rather as exchange—for I did not care for Redegonde—he would have said done. However, I did not, and I am glad of it. Even now, when a hundred thousand francs would be a fortune to me, I never repent of my delicacy.

After we had breakfasted merrily together, I told him that I liked him well, but that in the first place it would be well to ascertain whether the two commodities would consent to change masters.

"I am sure of Redegonde's consent," said Lord Percy.

"But I am not at all sure of Agatha's," said I.

"Why not?"

"I have very strong grounds for supposing that she would not consent to the arrangement. What reasons have you for the contrary opinion?"

"She will shew her sense."

"But she loves me."

"Well, Redegonde loves me."

"I dare say; but does she love me?"

"I am sure I don't know, but she will love you."

"Have you consulted her upon the point?"

"No, but it is all the same. What I want to know now is whether you approve of my plan, and how much you want for the exchange, for your Agatha is worth much more than my Redegonde."

"I am delighted to hear you do my mistress justice. As for the money question, we will speak of that later. In the first place I will take Agatha's opinion, and will let you know the result to-morrow morning."

The plan amused me, and though I was passionately attached to Agatha I knew my inconstant nature well enough to be aware that another woman, may be not so fair as she, would soon make me forget her. I therefore resolved to push the matter through if I could do so in a manner that would be advantageous for her.

What surprised me was that the young nobleman had gained possession of Redegonde, whose mother appeared so intractable, but I knew what an influence caprice has on woman, and this explained the enigma.

Agatha came to supper as usual, and laughed heartily when I told her   of
Lord Percy's proposal.

"Tell me," said I, "if you would agree to the change?"

"I will do just as you like," said she; "and if the money he offers be acceptable to you, I advise you to close with him."

I could see by the tone of her voice that she was jesting, but her reply did not please me. I should have liked to have my vanity flattered by a peremptory refusal, and consequently I felt angry. My face grew grave, and Agatha became melancholy.

"We will see," said I, "how it all ends."

Next day I went to breakfast with the Englishman, and told him Agatha was willing, but that I must first hear what Redegonde had to say.

"Quite right," he observed.

"I should require to know how we are to live together."

"The four of us had better go masked to the first ball at the Carignan Theatre. We will sup at a house which belongs to me, and there the bargain can be struck."

The party took place according to agreement, and at the given signal we all left the ball-room. My lord's carriage was in waiting, and we all drove away and got down at a house I seemed to know. We entered the hall, and the first thing I saw was the Corticelli. This roused my choler, and taking Percy aside I told him that such a trick was unworthy of a gentleman. He laughed, and said he thought I should like her to be thrown in, and that two pretty women were surely worth as much as Agatha. This amusing answer made me less angry; but, calling him a madman, I took Agatha by the arm and went out without staying for any explanations. I would not make use of his carriage, and instead of returning to the ball we went home in sedan-chairs, and spent a delicious night in each other's arms.

The End

www.ingramcontent.com/pod-product-compliance
Lightning Source LLC
Chambersburg PA
CBHW070119010626
45794CB00012B/288